The Messiah Project

The
Messiah
Project

JEFFERY LEE LEMIRE, SR.

CHAPTER 1

Doc Lucas was dead. I was still sitting in my chair holding the phone after receiving the call. Even though it was not unexpected, it still shocked me. He was ninety-seven years old after all. He never seemed that old, though. His mind was still the best one in any room that he occupied. The call was from his grandson, Jim, who was helping to make the funeral arrangements. They were asking me to speak at his funeral, which was a high honor, a surprise, and a bit intimidating. Doc Lucas had been friends with some of the best known theologians and Bible scholars in the country. Why they would want me to speak at his funeral I did not know. It was just the eulogy; I was not giving the funeral address. To be sure, over the years we had become very close. He had been my favorite prof in college. After college our ways had parted for several years then we crossed paths again a few years later when we were both involved in working at the same Bible camp in Idaho. He had been the Bible study teacher, and I was the youth worker. Funny how things happen.

During the course of that camp, we had become very close. There were hours of discussions covering everything from theology to prophecy to UFOs. He was very much "old-fashioned" in his thinking, but he was one of the few from his generation of theologians, to my knowledge, that thought that there could be life on other planets. That came as a surprise to me. It was the first of many. At first, I was very careful not to disagree with him, but by the end of the ten-day camp, we were having lively debates that both stimulated and challenged both of us. I don't mean to presume that I challenged his great mind. Those were his words. During the ten days of that camp, my life was changed forever, because "Doc," as we all referred to him, went from being just my mentor to being my friend as well. He also called me friend, which is still one of the highest honors of my life.

In August of that same year, I received a package in the mail with five books from Dr. Lucas's library and an invitation to spend the week between Christmas and New Year's with him at his home in West Virginia. He had bought a very old stone church and rectory near Fairmont, West Virginia. It was built on the side of a hill, as is most everything in that part of the country. My response was to select five books from my library and send them to him with a note saying, "I'll be there." He never said so, but I think my response amused him. That turned into an annual pilgrimage. Every year we exchanged five books each, read them, and then spent a week discussing the books, the Bible, theology, philosophy, doctrine, and all kinds of theories of almost everything. For me, the week at Stone House and Stone Church was the highlight of the year. We always ended the week with a New Year's Eve service in his church. From the first year, we would both speak at the service, which ran from nine in the evening to midnight or later. Then we would say our goodbyes and each return to our routines.

Over the years his activities went from a full schedule of teaching and preaching to being the senior pastor and then executive pastor of Stone Church. It was, by the way, one of the loveliest churches and parsonage combinations that I have seen anywhere. It was all native stone from the area. The sanctuary would seat around six hundred on the main floor and balcony. The rectory was well-appointed, being elegant without making a point of being expensive. The house was three stories with lots of bedrooms and bathrooms. My favorite room was the library, which was on the first floor just off the master suite. It was located at the back of the house, and the back wall of the library butted up against the mountain side. It was a fairly large room with a high ceiling. The walls were covered with built-in book cases. The walls were paneled with some elegant, dark wood paneling. There was a large fireplace and several reading tables. There was a ladder that was attached to a track so that it could be moved around the room to access the higher shelves. "Doc's" library was a thing of beauty to a person with a thirst for knowledge. He had also equipped it with a couple of computers so that research could be done using sources outside the library without leaving Stone House.

The funeral was to be held in the church, which seemed appropriate. He had been there for over forty years. He had hired associate pastors to assist him when he had to be away and then as his health and energy levels deteriorated with age. I don't know much about the heritage of the church before Doc Lucas bought it, but the heritage since was of the richest sort. Well-known teachers and evangelists from all over the world had graced the pulpit. There were audio and video tapes all around the world of addresses that had gone forth from that pulpit. To be sure the heritage was a rich one.

Now he was gone. Life would not be the same without "The Doc." His grandson that called had made a strange request. He asked that I make myself available for a few days after the burial. I told him that I would do so. I had about a month with no special commitments. My plans were to do some fishing, but I would probably still be able to work that in too.

I called the travel agency that I normally use to find another surprise. The airfare was already paid. My flight was to leave at ten thirty the next morning. I would fly into Pittsburg. Doc Lucas's grandson would meet me there and drive down into West Virginia. I just needed to pack a bag, which I did.

Throughout the afternoon and evening, my thoughts kept returning to conversations with Doc Lucas over the years. His mind was a beautiful thing. His grasp of historical, philosophical, theological, cosmological, and just plain practical concepts and how they connected and interacted never ceased to amaze me. One time we were discussing 2 Corinthians 5:17–21, and he said to me one of the keys to understanding that passage was to realize that Christ died for our sins to be sure, but more than that, he died *in our sins*. That statement nearly took my breath away. At the end of that visit, Doc Lucas preached from that passage during the New Year's Eve service. I was glad that I had spoken before him, because to try to follow that message would have been demoralizing. It was a theological and scriptural work of art in my humble opinion. His words still ring in my ears as though he just spoke them to me moments ago. He said, "Jesus died for our sins, but more than that, he died in our sins. In the garden, he began to drink the bitter cup that only he was able to drink. He began to be burdened with the sins and the sin of all men from the beginning to the end of time. He was then arrested, betrayed by a friend, and abandoned by his followers. He was tried and convicted by false witnesses. He was stripped naked and scourged. He was mocked and despised. Isaiah said, 'Surely he has borne our sorrows and carried our grief…he was wounded for our transgressions, he was bruised for our iniquities, the chastisement of our peace was upon him and with his stripes *we* are healed.' He did not speak to defend himself. He did not try to escape or avoid what was coming. He was there to do his Father's will. He died in our sins.

"He was placed in a grave, but that was not the end. Don't think for a moment that there was nothing redemptive taking place while the body of Jesus lay in the grave. His soul was cast into Satan's dungeon just like any other sinner. In fact, he was the not only one who came in that day. All over the world people were dying and being cast into the place of death. There were two thieves that were crucified on either side of Jesus that were there. But there was something different about this one. Satan was accustomed to seeing sinners cast into hell with their load of sin. Some came with more baggage than others, but this one came with a load of sin like nobody had ever seen. Some have speculated about the party that was going on in the regions of the damned when Jesus died. Maybe that is true, but the party didn't last very long. If you'll allow me some license here, I think that when Satan and the hosts of hell saw the load of sin that Jesus brought in there, they were astonished. I believe Satan walked slowly around Jesus and surveyed the crushing mountain of sin of every kind. I would speculate that the question spontaneously came out from him, 'Who is this man? We thought we killed the Lord of Glory, but who is this sinner?' Then he turned to Jesus and demanded of him, 'Who are you?' Now Jesus had stood silently before his accusers, while on trial, but he was silent no more! As he stood alone in the presence of Satan and all his minions, the sin with which he was laden began to slide off until he stood pure and untouched by it. Then he spoke. He said, 'I Am that I AM. I am the Root of Jesse; I am the Son of David. I am the Bright and the Morning Star; I am the Lamb of God which takes away the sin of the world and there it is [pointing to the load of sin that he had carried to this place]. I have taken them away. I am the conqueror of sin, death, and the grave. I am the King of Glory and there is none beside me. I am the King of kings and the Lord of lords! Give me the keys of death and the grave!'"

Doc Lucas went on to say, "Don't you know that there was pandemonium on the cell blocks? Abraham, Isaac, Jacob, Moses, David, Isaiah, Daniel, and all of those who had died in the faith not having seen the promise were shouting out things like, 'I know that voice!' 'It's him; he has come!' The cells were thrown open and a procession, not unlike the Israelites leaving Egypt, was forming. He led them out of that place. Again you need to allow me some latitude here, but I think King David, the Sweet Singer of Israel, led the singing as they marched out. If I could choose a psalm that would be appropriate I think I would choose Psalm 24 verses 7 through 10: 'Lift up your heads, O ye gates! And be lifted up ye everlasting doors! And the King of Glory shall come in! Who is this King of Glory? The Lord strong and mighty, The Lord mighty in battle. Lift up your heads, O ye gates! Lift up, ye everlasting doors! And the King of Glory shall come in! Who is this King of Glory? The Lord of hosts, He is the King of Glory!' He led them into the place of his rest and the glory of his presence.

"All of this took place outside of the view of men on earth. Then on the first day of the week, the stone was rolled away so that the world could see that he was not dead, but risen. The stone was not rolled away to let Jesus out, but to let the witnesses in. They testified to a risen Lord, and their testimony comes down to us today. We still believe in a crucified and risen Redeemer. Please allow me to wrap this up with this thought. Verse 21 of this passage says that he who knew no sin was made to be sin for us that we might be made the righteousness of God in him. Please consider my paraphrase of this verse. I believe that I do no damage to the meaning. Jesus took our sins upon himself as though they were his own so that we might be clothed in the righteousness of God in Christ as though it were our own."

I will not forget that message as long as I live. It has inspired me more times that I can count on all of my fingers and toes. There was no better preacher than Doc Lucas when he was inspired. He would certainly be missed. What I wouldn't give for one more conversation with him. There is no doubt in my mind that he has forgotten more than I will ever know.

During our annual meetings, Doc Lucas had related that he was just fresh out of seminary when the United States entered World War II. He was married and had one child. He had been appointed to a good church in Pennsylvania. It looked like his life was starting out perfectly. Then he felt strongly impressed to join the Military Chaplain Corp. His wife was upset, his church leaders were upset, but he felt that if his countrymen were fighting and dying on foreign soil, they needed somebody there who could point them in the right direction. He joined the Navy Chaplain Corp and was assigned to a Marine Combat Division. He spent much of WWII in the trenches with men who were fighting and dying. He had some stories that would be unbelievable from somebody else. He wrapped his war experience up in one sentence. He said, "I never felt more needed in my life, before or since." That said a lot about him. He had a strong sense of duty. He always tried to go where he was needed. In a sense, he never stopped taking marching orders. He always considered himself a soldier of the cross. In fact, one of his recurring words of advice was just that. He said repeatedly to me, "Press the case for the cross, son, press the cross."

Tomorrow I would be travelling to his funeral.

CHAPTER 2

The flight touched down in Pittsburg right on schedule. When I saw Jim Lucas, I knew him immediately although we had never actually met. I had seen photos of him at Doc Lucas's home. It was hard to mistake him. He looked like a younger, slightly taller version of his grandfather. I told him so when I met him. He was gratified that I thought that he looked like his grandfather. His grandfather's full name was James David Lucas. Time had shortened it to JD. I asked Jim if he was now going be the JD Lucas of the world. I really liked his answer. He said, "There was only one JD Lucas. Nobody could ever take his place and nobody should ever take his title. I'll always be Jimmy or Jim. That's good enough for me." There was great admiration in this young man for his grandfather. That scored him points in my book. He looked quite athletic, so I asked him about it. He had played both football and baseball in high school and college. He said there were major league scouts looking at him, but he discussed it with his grandfather who encouraged him to seek a higher calling. He did and said that he did not regret it. I told him about Doc Lucas's seventy-fifth birthday party. We played a game of pick-up softball. Doc Lucas pitched for one of the teams and took his turn at bat. He didn't run the bases though. He had one of the young bucks to that for him. He went three for three that day and had a couple of put-outs at first base. Jim laughed at that story. He said that in some ways I knew him better than his family did. I didn't say anything to that, but reflected on what a shame it is.

We walked out to Jim's car. He mentioned the heat, but for me, coming in from Houston, it felt like spring. July in Houston is not for the weak. The air felt fresh and very nice to me as we walked to the car. On the way out of Pittsburg, we stopped and ate a quick lunch. Although not very hungry, I was able to eat a salad and a couple of pepperoni rolls. They're something that we don't have in Texas. They're sort of a specialty in West Virginia and southern Pennsylvania. They look like a dinner roll, but have pepperoni rolled up inside. They are delicious. It may a specialty from the Italian culture. I'm really not sure about that.

Over lunch we discussed several things, the funeral being one of them. Jim told me that there were several family members already there and more coming. All of Doc's living children were already there, so I would be able to chat with them to put together a eulogy. I also found that we were all staying at Stone House. Apparently there was room for everyone there. It seemed that I would not have to rent a car for the time that I was there. The drive to West Virginia from Pittsburg was a really beautiful drive. It seemed that Mother Nature had put on her best dress for the occasion. Just north of Morgantown, I dozed off and awakened when we pulled off the expressway in Fairmont. I apologized for falling asleep on him, and he just laughed. He said that his mother had called while we were driving and would like to meet with me later this afternoon, if possible. I told him that it would be fine. We arrived at Stone House at around four thirty.

When we arrived at Stone House there was another shock awaiting me. I had met all of Doc's living children over the years. We had always been very friendly, but now they greeted me like a long-lost brother. There were hugs and tears all around. Since confession is said to be good for the soul, I must confess that I shed a few of my own for my own loss, but for theirs as well. One surprise was that Doc had planned his own funeral and he had personally requested that I give the eulogy. The other really big surprise was that, on Doc Lucas's orders, I was to stay in the master suite. I tried to protest, but they would not hear of it. It was the doctor's orders, so to speak. While all this was going on, I noticed a look from youngest brother, Steve. If looks could kill, I would have been in the box next to Doc Lucas. I didn't give it much thought at the time, but neither did I forget it.

I spent a couple of hours chatting with the family taking notes and recording the conversations for later reference. I caught up with Steve near the end of the time with the family. He told me several stories about his dad. Most of his stories had to do with his dad being gone so much when he was young. There was almost a tangible force of suppressed anger coming from him. It seemed curious to me. I found that he had a doctorate in history and taught at Boston College. He was married, with two sons and a daughter. His family was not able to come to the funeral. He did not seem particularly regretful that his family did not come. Everyone else had their entire family there. It seemed a bit odd to me, but at the time, I gave it no thought. The funeral was at eleven the next morning, and we still needed to go for visitation at the funeral home this evening. I ate a quick bite of dinner and changed to go to the funeral home.

The funeral home was overflowing with colleagues, former students, friends, and well-wishers. There were more preachers present that I have ever seen in one place in my life. I was reasonably sure that the church would be very crowded tomorrow morning. I chatted with several people that I had known over the years. Several of my classmates from the years spent in college were there. It was nice to reconnect with them. A few of us stood together and reminisced about Doc Lucas and what he had taught us. We all agreed that he had influenced our lives more than he had known. They all treated me differently than they ever had before. There was a certain deference or something that I couldn't put my finger on. Finally my old friend, Danny Jensen, who I hadn't seen for about five years, took me aside. He said, "You don't know what is going on here, do you?"

I replied, "I have no idea what you are talking about."

He said, "Don't you know what Doc Lucas thought of you?"

I said, "We were great friends and very close. As far as I know he thought of me as his friend."

Danny replied, "For a smart guy, you certainly can be dumb sometimes."

I looked at him and smiled. "What are you talking about?"

Danny said, "Doc Lucas thought that you were the brightest student that he ever taught. He has been grooming you as his protégé!"

I was flabbergasted and told him, "You are out of your mind."

He replied, "I guess he told everybody but you. It's to your credit that you never even thought it to be the case. I'm thinking he chose well."

I was so shocked that I didn't know what to say. I told Danny, "I need to leave. I have no idea what you're talking about and I need to think. Can you run me over to Stone House? I didn't rent a car when I got here."

He said, "Sure thing, let's go."

We drove slowly over to Doc's house. It wasn't very far, and I'm afraid that I didn't have much to say. When he dropped me off at the house, he said, "You really didn't see this coming, did you?"

Again I was confused. "See what coming? Doc was ninety-seven years old. I've been expecting this for several years now."

"I don't mean his death," he responded.

"Well, what do you mean then, Danny? I don't get it!" I said.

Then he dropped the bombshell. "Doc is giving you the keys to the kingdom. You are his intellectual heir apparent!"

Now, I really had no words. I stared at him and mumbled, "Good night, Danny," and walked away with him laughing at me. I didn't know if I would get a wink of sleep tonight.

I went to my room and spent an hour or so going over the notes that I had made while visiting with Doc Lucas's family and friends. It felt like I was making some headway on what I wanted to say. This kind of thing could turn on a dime, though. In the morning, I could look at what I was jotting down this evening and not like any of it. It was making sense tonight though.

I was starting to feel sleepy. I pulled down the covers and slid into bed. As my hand slipped under the pillow, I felt something underneath it. I had not turned the bedside light off, so I pulled out what I found under the pillow. It was an envelope with my name on it: Jack Spencer. It was addressed in Doc's handwriting. I opened it up and found one sheet of paper and a bunch of keys. In Doc's handwriting were these simple words.

Jack,

I have prayed much and thought hard about what would become of Stone Church when I leave this world. I am leaving it all to you. I have already given my children and grandchildren everything of my personal possessions that I want them to have. Everything here including the church building and contents and Stone House and its contents are yours. I put no strings on it, but it is my hope that you will live here and continue my work and research. If you do so, you will make an old teacher very happy. God bless you, my friend and son in the faith. Remember when all else fails, "Press the cross, son, press the cross!"

Doc

To say that I was stunned would qualify as the understatement of my lifetime. I was in such a state of shock that my brain wouldn't work. I was hearing a sound for several seconds before I realized that my phone was ringing. I picked up my cell phone and answered it. The voice on the other end was familiar, but I couldn't place it. The voice said, "Did I wake you?"

I replied, "No, I wasn't asleep yet." The voice on the other end identified itself as Bill Wagner, Dr. Lucas's attorney. "Your timing could not be more appropriate. I just read a note from Dr. Lucas that has my head swimming."

Bill chuckled, "They say that timing is everything. So you have read the note from Dr. Lucas?"

"Yes, I have," I replied. "It's good that you called because I was on the verge of an old-fashioned freak-out."

Again Bill chuckled, "Doc Lucas told me that you were one of the most unassuming people he had ever met. That was high praise coming from him. Look, could we meet tomorrow morning before the funeral?"

I replied, "Maybe we could have breakfast together; I almost always eat on schedule."

"That sounds good," he replied; "Why don't you meet me and the IHOP on 14th Street at around eight thirty? That way we can talk and be back in time for the funeral with no problems."

I responded, "It's a date, see you then."

When I met Bill Wagner I was a little bit surprised because he was so young. He didn't look old enough to be out of high school, let alone law school. He must have seen my skepticism because he started grinning. His first words were, "Believe it or not, I am dry behind the ears."

"That's a relief," I responded. "You don't look old enough to have completed law school and passed the bar, but then everybody looks young to me. What's good to eat here?"

He said, "Everything, but I usually have the harvest grain pancakes." He ordered his pancakes, and I ordered a veggie omelet with rye toast. While we waited for our food, Bill got right down to business. He told me that the oversight of the church came with a decent stipend of $120,000.00 per year, which exacerbated my already surprised condition. There would be a new car every two years. Doc Lucas's almost new Caddy was mine, and he told me where to find the keys. I had borrowed a car from one of Doc's family this morning. He also told me that Doc wanted me to finish a book that he had about half finished. "I'm not qualified to do that!" I told him. He responded, "Doc Lucas thought that you are.

I tend to trust his evaluation of people more than anybody else that I know. If he says that you can do it, you can do it." He also advised that the ministry staff would remain in place as long as I wanted them.

Our food came, and neither one of us talked for a while. Once we polished off our breakfast, Bill asked me, "What do you think?"

My response was, "I can't think right now. I need to process."

His now familiar chuckle came again. "Doc said that you would say that. He knew you pretty well, you know," he said.

"It is my sincerest hope that he knew me better than I think I know myself. I feel like a lion in a den of Daniel's right now," was my response. At that he laughed right out loud. It was nine thirty, and I wanted to get back to the church to put the finishing touches on the eulogy. We agreed to meet in the next few days. He told me that I would need to be available for the reading of the will. I told him that I was planning on staying the week or longer if necessary.

When I got back to Stone House, I went to my room to prepare for the funeral. I touched up the eulogy and then wandered over to the church. I was about forty-five minutes early, but wanted to spend some time meditating before people began to gather. Doc's body was already on display. He looked good; he surely didn't look ninety-seven years old. I remembered him telling me when he turned eighty that if he had known he was going to live so long, he would have taken better care of himself. It looked to me like he had taken pretty good care of himself. I wandered up to the balcony and sat in a quiet corner. I went over my notes and jotted down a couple of more little things that I thought that I might add. It was ten forty-five, and the church was filling up fast. I walked down to where the family was gathering. There were more hugs and tears as the family realized that this really was goodbye. I was handed a schedule of service, which showed me when I was to stand up and speak. The rest was pretty much a blur to me. I had way too much on my mind right now to focus.

The service started right on schedule. Doc would have been proud. The music was superb. Doc always had great taste in music. His funeral was no exception. After a couple of songs and a couple of family members speaking, my turn came. I stood up and surveyed the church, which was filled to overflowing and then some. I started. "James David Lucas lived ninety-seven years on this earth. He entered into a personal relationship with his God as a young man and walked with him for over eighty years. He was a man who always chose the right, if he could figure out what it was. Did he make mistakes? Yes. Not as many as most of us nor were they as serious as many of ours. He was a husband, father, pastor, teacher, Bible scholar, theologian, philosopher, historian, mentor, and many other things. To me, he was a great friend. He lived by words that are, for many people today, out of style. He lived by faith, commitment, duty, and words like that. His life was more than just a series of days waiting to die. He wanted every day of his life to count for something significant. I wondered why he wanted me to do this. After thinking about it, I believe that I understand. Many knew him in the role or roles he played in their lives. Few knew him just as a man who was searching for answers and vulnerable before his God. If Doc Lucas could write his own eulogy, he would probably say that he was just an unprofitable servant. Whatever he accomplished in his life was merely doing his duty. He was a servant of God, and all the good that came of his life and ministry came from the hand of God. He would not glory in his life or his accomplishments; he would glory in the cross of Christ. In fact that was his favorite hymn, number 42 in the Hymn Book.

In the Cross of Christ I glory,

Towering o're the wrecks of time.

All the light of sacred glory

Gathers 'round its head sublime.

When the woes of life o'er take me,

Hopes deceive and fears annoy,

Never shall the cross forsake me.

Lo! It glows with peace and joy.

When the sun of bliss is beaming,

Light and love upon my way,

From the cross the radiance streaming,

Adds more luster to the day.

Bane and blessing, pain and pleasure

By the cross are sanctified.

Peace there is that knows no measure,

Joys that thro'all time abide.

"That was the favorite hymn of James David Lucas. He found peace and joy at the cross. He lived for the cross, and he died serving the Christ of the cross. Little more needs to be said of this fine man that we lay to rest today. God bless you all and God bless the memory and legacy of James David Lucas."

I then sat down and heard very little of the rest of the service. My mind was overwhelmed by memories of conversations with Doc, messages I had heard him preach, and books we had read and analyzed together. These were truly precious memories. When the service ended, we were ushered to the fellowship hall where an incredible dinner had been prepared by the ladies of Stone Church. They were paying their last tribute to their pastor of so many years, and a fitting tribute it was. Even though there were hundreds of people in attendance, I had my doubts that we would be able to put a dent in the mountain of food that was pile on the serving tables.

As we ate, I found myself seated beside one of Doc's daughters, Sally. In fact, she was the mother of Jim, the grandson who had picked me up at the airport. She had maneuvered her way to sit beside me. She said, "I have been wanting to talk with you ever since you arrived, but there just has not been time. It seems in his later years, you knew Dad better than anyone else with the exception of his secretary, Jennifer."

My response was, "Well, I don't know about that. Your father and I had our annual get-together, and we spoke on the phone about once a month."

She said, "He spoke more highly of you than anyone else other than family. In fact, although he never said so, I think he secretly wished you were his son too."

That came as a surprise to me, but I covered and responded, "He came to be my best friend as the years rolled by. He never ridiculed an idea that I had, and there were some really outlandish ones. He always acted like every idea had merit and should be considered. He never made me feel stupid, even though I'm sure that I was sometimes."

She replied, "I don't think he ever thought that about you. I've heard him say that about some people like their ideas were the most preposterous thing he had ever heard, but he never said that about you. Come to think of it, I don't recall ever hearing him discuss the things that he discussed with you. It was like it was his own private place and he did not want to share it."

"To tell you the truth, some of the things we talked about were so 'out there' that to discuss them outside of the context of our discussions might have sounded a bit nutty," I replied.

"Like what?" she asked.

I answered, "Trust me, it would not make good dinner conversation."

"Maybe some other time then?" she asked.

My reply was, "We'll see what happens." Then she asked if I was staying for a few days, and I replied that I was planning to do so. I then said my goodbyes and left for Stone House.

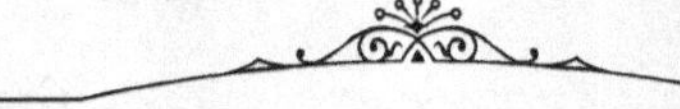

CHAPTER 3

I was really tired. I had not slept much last night, and the events of today had been emotionally taxing. My room looked just like I had left it. I stretched out on the bed thinking that I would relax for a few minutes.

A sound in the library adjacent to the bedroom awakened me. Somebody was moving around in there. I walked to the door and was about to open it when I saw there was a peep hole in the door so that I could look into the library without opening the door. I looked through the hole, but could not see the entire room. Then stepping from the blind spot of the peep hole was Steve Lucas, Doc's youngest son. Since I saw no threat there, I opened the door and stepped into the room. The door opened so quietly, that Steve did not realize that I was in the room. He appeared to be looking for something. I spoke to him and nearly scared him out of his skin, "Can I help you find something, Steve?" I asked.

His feet left the floor, and he spun around to face me. The look on his face was one of guilt like a kid caught stealing a cookie. His face changed almost instantly from fear to anger to calm. I was impressed with his ability to cover his feelings. "Oh, Jack!" he said. "I did not want to disturb you."

I asked the obvious question, "What are you looking for?"

"My dad promised me a couple of books on the Roman Empire. I was just looking for them," he replied.

I remembered Doc's note under my pillow and doubted that Steve was telling the truth. I had also noted that he was rummaging through papers in and on the desk. I asked him, "Do you think that he left them in his desk?"

He looked at me, his face unchanged, but his eyes hated me. It would be wise to remember those eyes. They were not kind and did not convey benevolent feelings toward me. It was also worth noting that he had come in after hours when Jennifer, Doc's secretary, would be gone. I decided to poke the bear again, "You should probably ask Jennifer. If the books are around here, she would know. Knowing your father as I did, he probably packed them up and placed them somewhere for you."

He responded, "I'll ask her in the morning." Then he walked out of the library without another word or a backward glance.

Since the only entrances to the library were from the hallway and my suite, I locked the door to the hallway and went back to my room. Steve was not going to be my friend; that much was clear.

The next morning I went down to the dining room to have some breakfast. Dr. Lucas's oldest son, Michael, was there with

Bill Wagner. Bill and Michael were glad I was there as they had wanted to speak with me. Michael thanked me for the eulogy. He expressed that his father would have been pleased. Bill thought so too. Bill told me that the reading of the will would be at three that afternoon in his office. My response was, "I was planning on going down to the river to do a little fishing anyway, so that's fine."

Michael interjected, "You need to be there for the reading of the will."

"Whatever for?" I asked.

"Because it was my father's wish," he replied.

I responded, "There are some in your family who will not want me there."

"You mean Steve; he has underestimated you. He did not think that you detected his animosity," replied Michael.

"Frankly, it was hard to miss," I replied, smiling back at him.

He smiled back at me and said, "I can see why Dad liked you so well. You remind me of him."

"Wow!" I answered, "I'm not sure what to do with that."

"You don't need to do anything with it. It is what it is," was his response. Bill spoke up then and said that he needed to get back to his office. "See you at three o'clock," and he was gone.

Michael and I each had another cup of coffee. We didn't say anything more as we both seemed to be lost in our own thoughts. I finished my coffee and got up to return to my room. Before leaving I asked Michael, "Do you know where there are a couple of books on the Roman Empire that your father was planning to give to Steve?"

He looked at me with a puzzled look. "He gave those books to Steve a month ago. I happened to be here and saw Steve place them in his car."

I responded, "I must have misunderstood. See you later."

As I walked back to my suite, I had much to ponder. Why would Steve lie to me? What was he really looking for? What was I getting myself into here? I tried to enter the library from the hallway and found it locked. I recalled that I had locked it last night when Steve awakened me with his rummaging around. As I passed Jennifer's office I saw that she was there. She and her husband had worked for Dr. Lucas for twenty-five years. She was the doctor's personal secretary, and he kept the grounds and did maintenance on the buildings. They had been newly married and twenty years old when they came here. I stepped in and said, "Good morning, Jennifer. How are you holding up?"

She looked up, and her eyes were red from crying. "It's really hard. I worked for Dr. Lucas for the last twenty-five years. He was like a father to me."

"I know," I said. "He thought the world of you too. I am so sorry for your loss."

That brought a new flood of tears. She sobbed out. "Nobody else, other than my husband, has said anything to me like that. Thank you for that."

"By the way, did Steve ask you for access to the library to look for some books that his father apparently promised to him?" I asked.

She replied, "Dr. Lucas gave him those books a month ago. I distinctly remember. He told me that nothing else was to be removed from his office until you arrived."

"What does that mean?" I asked.

She looked at me with a sly look in her eye and asked, "You did get the note that Dr. Lucas told me to put under your pillow, didn't you?"

"Yes, I did. Did you read it?" I asked.

"No, but Dr. Lucas told me that when you arrive, you would be in charge and everything in the library was to be preserved just has he left it for you. I guess we'll find out what is going on at the reading of the will this afternoon," she responded.

My parting comment was, "I guess you are right about that." I then went into my room. As I entered my room, I was thinking that Doc must have had some premonition of his demise to make such specific preparations.

I made a quick call to my fishing partner and made arrangements to spend next week in Michigan fishing for small mouth bass. I love to float those Michigan rivers fishing for small mouth. Mike, my fishing buddy, told me that it looked like the conditions would be perfect next week. Now I had something to look forward to for the rest of this week. I then went into the library. It was a familiar place. Dr. Lucas and I had spent many an hour seated before the fireplace or at one of the various desks or tables discussing theories and points of whatever topic we were wearing out on that particular day. We would spread our books on the desks and tables and go at it for hours on end. I looked around the room. Doc had decorated his library with a collection of crosses. He had carved crosses, sculptured crosses, painted crosses, bejeweled crosses, plain crosses, mirrored crosses, braided crosses. You name it and he had it. I would not change anything in this room. There were twelve inlaid crosses in the wood work of the fireplace. It was really a work of art. According to Dr. Lucas, it was there before he bought the place. It was part of the original structure. Much of Stone House had been remodeled, but the library had not been touched. I would not change it either. It was one of a kind. To change it would be to spoil it. Far be it from me to do that.

I sat down at the huge desk that had been the personal and private perch of Dr. James David Lucas for over forty years. He had become commonly known as JD Lucas. Most people across the country knew him by that title. Only a few knew him as Doc and fewer still could call him James. He had bestowed that honor upon me, but I only used his first name when we were in private. It felt unseemly to use it when others were around. I think Michael was the only one of his children who had ever heard me speak to his father using his first name. Michael knew the close bond between his father and me.

As I sat there I pondered how by different paths life had landed two very different men of different generations at the same desk. Both of us had an above average thirst for knowledge. We both were willing to search in unconventional places for pieces of a puzzle. We both had served in the military. He served in the chaplain corps; I served in Special Forces. He always felt that the training received in the military served me well in other pursuits as well. That was probably true. One thing that we really had in common is that we both were willing to think outside the box if the line of thought was not contrary to scripture. That was the anchor for both of us. We did not want to play outside of the parameters set by the Bible. Having said that, all of factual history was fair game for our queries. The real tough nut to crack was prophecy. We had discussed Revelation, Daniel, Ezekiel, Matthew 24, and various other prophetic writings at length. Like most, we still had more questions than answers. We were aware that much of our ideas were speculation and had agreed that we would not discuss them outside of this library until we had some concrete evidence presented itself that would support our speculation with fact. So far, most of our thoughts were in a secret place that only Doc knew about. I wondered if he had left me a hint as to where he had hidden our research. It was my plan to look for it, but not today. We had to attend the reading of the will at Bill Wagner's office this afternoon.

I noticed that it was after one in the afternoon and I had not had any lunch. In fact, until right now, I had not noticed that I was hungry. I went down to the kitchen. There was food left over from the after-the-funeral dinner yesterday. I found some ham and made a sandwich. Then I scrounged up some salad and found the dressing to go with it. While I was eating, the house was quiet. Maybe the others were out shopping or whatever before going to Bill's office. Quiet didn't bother me. It was nice after the last couple of days. As I walked back toward the master suite, I noticed a couple of cars setting in the driveway. They were loaded to the gills with stuff from the house. I didn't want to make enemies of the doctor's family, so I just called Bill and asked him if he had authorized anybody to take anything from the house, as he, Bill, was the executor of the will. He said that he had not, but would look into it. I went into the master suite and settled down in the office again. It was around one thirty. I heard a bit of commotion going on outside, but did not pay any attention to it. I suspected that Bill had made a couple of phone calls. It didn't really matter to me if Doc's kids took some of his stuff. It just wasn't their place to loot the house before the will was read. I had asked Bill not to let anyone know that I was the one who had tipped him off. It looked like the family might be going to the reading of the will with their boxing gloves on.

I arrived at the attorney's office at two fifty-five. There was no good reason to be early. I did not know what to expect, but was not expecting much. I figured the position at the church was the bulk of what I could expect and really was more than I had expected. That came as a big surprise to me.

Bill ushered us into his largest conference room. There were seats for all. After a few general comments, the reading of the will began. There were monies and properties divided up between the children. I had no idea that Doc was so well-off, but it should not have been surprising. He had about twenty-five books in print, and many of them were reprinted and continued to be strong-selling books. Finally the reading was finished. I had not been mentioned as was wondering why I was even there. Steve spoke up and asked, "What about Stone Church and Stone House? They weren't mentioned in the will."

Bill looked up and replied, "I was coming to that. It has already been deeded to the new owner. The property and all contents not previously given by Dr. Lucas or mentioned in the will are now the property of Jack Spencer. This transfer took place about two years before Dr. Lucas's passing." There was silence in the room for longer than was comfortable for me. Bill went on, "I have a complete inventory of the items that should be in the house, church, and outbuildings. Nothing should be removed that was not previously given to you by your father. None of the property in the house, church, outbuildings, and on the grounds belongs to the family of James David Lucas anymore. If you were planning on taking anything, you should clear it with Jack. I have all of the paperwork here, in case you do not believe me." Bill looked at me and said, "Do you have any questions or comments?"

I told him, "I have to think this through. I had no idea this was coming. I can hardly breathe right now!"

Michael came over and laid his hand on my shoulder. "He told me he was going to do this Doc and asked me what I thought. I told him it was his choice, but I could not think of a better successor for him here at Stone Church and Stone House. Congratulations!"

I stood up and reached for his hand thanking him for his generous spirit. I then said to all of the Lucases who were present, "You are all welcome to come and stay at Stone House as often and as long as you like. Other than that, I am at a loss for words. What do you say at a moment like this? Bill, that invitation includes you. I want to retain you as my attorney for whatever work needs to be done." He thanked me and said that he would come by tomorrow with papers to go over.

As I left Bill Wagner's office I had the strangest feeling. I looked over my shoulder and saw Steve Lucas once again staring at me with the most malevolent look in his eye. I did not understand why, but thought it wouldn't be a bad idea to clear the air, if the opportunity presented itself. It was five thirty when I arrived back at Stone House. When I walked in, Jennifer was still there. She asked me what had happened and I told her. She smiled and said, "I knew it! I just knew it!"

"Did Doc say something to you?" I asked.

"No," she replied, "I just figured it out."

"Well, one thing for sure," I said, "I want you to remain right where you are. You and your husband have your positions for as long as you want them, and I hope that you will stay."

"We have talked about it, and it is our hope that we can stay," she said.

"Then it's settled," I said. "Starting today, we will keep the library and the master suite locked. I saw somebody snooping around in the library last evening. I don't want anything disturbed until I have had a chance to sort things out."

"Okay," she said, "I'll keep it locked."

"Thanks, Jennifer. See you tomorrow."

I went into my suite and changed into a golf shirt. Then I went to the kitchen to grab a quick bite of dinner. I wasn't very hungry and found some fruit and yogurt. I cut up an apple, put in some grapes and peanuts. Then I mixed some salted peanuts in with some blueberry yogurt. Then I ate it. It was really tasty. After eating, I went into the library and started going through the papers and files that Doc had left for me. I worked until about ten thirty and then just went to bed. I was worn out. It had been quite a day. It was not until I went to bed that I realized that none of the Lucas family other than Michael had said a word to me since the reading of the will. I remember wondering if that meant anything…then oblivion settled over me.

CHAPTER 4

I was awakened just as the sky began to brighten by the birds singing outside my window. Even though the window was closed, I could hear them announcing the dawn of another day. I walked over and opened the window. I could see the valley spread out before me. The bell tower of the Catholic Church was about a quarter of a mile down the hill. Because Stone House was nearly at the top of the hill, the tower of the church was about level with the front entrance of Stone House. The entrance was to the left of where I was standing on the same level. The view was spectacular in the early morning. It looked like it was going to be a nice day.

I went looking for coffee and found a pot in the library. There was some coffee there. There was a sink with water available right there, so I went ahead and started a pot of coffee. After a quick shower, the coffee was ready, so I started my day the way I most always did, sipping coffee in the early morning light. One thing that Doc Lucas and I had agreed on was that there is something very satisfying about routine. I sat down near one of the windows with my coffee and Bible. The passage for that day was from *Isaiah 55:6–9, "Seek ye the LORD while he may be found, call ye upon him while he is near: Let the wicked forsake his way, and the unrighteous man his thoughts: and let him return unto the LORD, and he will have mercy upon him; and to our God, for he will abundantly pardon. For my thoughts are not your thoughts, neither are your ways my ways, saith the LORD. For as the heavens are higher than the earth, so are my ways higher than your ways, and my thoughts than your thoughts"*

After reading this short passage, I sat back in my chair and closed my eyes and began to meditate on those words. Would we ever know the mind of God? Why does God do things the way he does? Why were some of my good friends killed in Vietnam and I was spared? How does God decide who gets to live out their lives and whose are cut short? How do such corrupted people get elected to office and good people left on the sidelines? There are so many questions that just don't have answers. My faith holds me to the belief that God is always good. He always knows the best course for us. If we follow him and his leadings, we will have the best life possible, if not the easiest. With the events of the last few days, this was a good place for me to be this morning. I suddenly noticed that I was hungry. Breakfast sounded like a good idea.

I walked down to the kitchen carrying my coffee. When I walked into the kitchen, Sally was there. She told me breakfast was ready and already set up in the dining room. When I walked into the dining room, all of the Lucas family was there. They were smiling and began to clap when I walked in. They all wanted to have breakfast with me before heading out. Every one of them shook my hand, and all of them, with the exception of Steve, wished me well. They thanked me for extending such a generous invitation to come to the house. I made sure that they understood that it was not just for show. They were welcome any time. Michael stood up and said, "I have been asked to speak for the family this morning. We know that our dad was a most particular person when it came to his friends. He must have really loved you to entrust his church and ministry to you. If you're good enough for him, you're good enough for us. We, as of last night, are making you an honorary Lucas. Welcome to the family, brother."

I was overwhelmed at the generous gesture. I tried to thank them as well as possible with the basketball in my throat. Then somebody yelled out, "I'm hungry!" and the moment was gone. We sat down and ate breakfast. There was a warmth in the room that morning that reminded me of some of the times with Doc. The Lucas girls had outdone themselves. There were heaps of food on the table. The girls knew their men, however. By the time that crowd assaulted the culinary beaches, there wasn't much left for the stragglers. I decided to file that away in the back of my bonnet in case I was ever invited for a Lucas family dinner. You'd better eat it while it's there because it won't be there for long.

After breakfast, they began saying their goodbyes. Several of them came to me asking for things that had belonged to their mother and/or dad. I held nothing back. The only room that I felt was off-limits was the library. Strangely enough, nobody asked for anything from the library. It was like they knew that their dad meant for me to have that sanctuary that had been his for my own. I did catch Steve and ask him if he had found the books that he was looking for yesterday. He mumbled something unintelligible and walked quickly away. By ten they were all gone.

When I got back to the library, there was a message on my phone from Bill Wagner. He said that he was coming by after lunch with some papers to sign and some things that Doc had not wanted to leave in the house. I called his office and spoke to his secretary and let her know that I would be expecting him. Then I checked with Jennifer to see if there was anything that required my attention. She said that there was not, so I began to go through some more of the files that I had found. Most of it was stuff that Doc Lucas had been working on. One of the files was a book Doc had been working on. It was about half done. There were instructions in the file for me to complete it. I remember thinking that it would be a cold day you know where before I would be able to finish a work that Doc Lucas had started. I started reading through the finished chapters and found myself mesmerized by them. It was almost like hearing his voice again. As the last finished chapter ended, Jennifer announced that Bill had arrived. I looked at the clock and it was one thirty. Where had the morning gone?

When Bill told me that he had some materials for me that Doc did not want to leave in the house, I thought maybe a briefcase of stuff. I should have known better. Bill came in rolling a two-wheel cart loaded with six boxes of papers. "What are you doing to me?" I asked him.

"I don't know what is in these boxes and I don't want to know," he said. "Doc said that this stuff is so private that he did not want it left in the house for his family to dig through. There's a safe in the floor here in the library. I'll show you how to open it and help you put it in there. You can go through this when you have the time." We loaded the boxes into the safe and then signed the papers needed to give my full ownership of the property. There were annual salaries for myself, Jennifer and her husband, the associate pastors and music leaders and custodians. These were all paid from Doc's estate.

Bill told me that the accounts were all mine now. He asked me if I wanted to make any changes and I told him, "Not now. I need to understand how all this works before I make any changes."

Bill smiled and said, "That's what Doc said you would say. He knew you pretty well." It was about three o'clock when we finished and Bill left. I sat back and tried to relax, but my mind was in a royal uproar. My brain would not stop spinning. I decided to take a walk to stretch my legs and maybe clear my mind a bit. I put the key to the safe around my neck and headed out.

As I stepped out onto the front porch, a swarm of mosquitos went for my head. Those are the only mosquitos that I will ever thank the Lord for, because as I ducked to avoid the mosquitos, something smashed into the porch post next to my head. I knew what it was before I even heard the report of the rifle. Somebody was shooting at me! Without even knowing that I had moved, I found myself under the bush to the left of the porch. I had put a stonewall between me and where I had heard the report of the shot. I had my cell phone in my hand too. I didn't remember getting that out. I called 911 and did not budge or raise my head until I heard the sirens and knew that the police were pulling into the drive coming up to Stone House.

The investigating officer was Sergeant Cooper. He was a smallish guy, but didn't look like a person that you would mess with. I related what had happened and how the mosquitos had caused me to move my head just a split second before the shot was fired. He was curious about my reaction. He said most people don't react so quickly or correctly. I told him that it was not the first time in my life that I had been shot at, although it was the first time outside of a war zone. I didn't divulge details of my military experience, much of which was classified and most of which you just don't talk about. It hadn't been pretty. That's for sure.

Sergeant Cooper asked if I had seen anything. I told him that I thought the muzzle flash came from the tower of the Catholic Church. It was about eye level with me when I came out the door. I had seen movement over there, but thought it was just birds in the tower. When I jerked my head back from the mosquitos, I caught the muzzle flash out of the corner of my eye. He asked if I was sure, and I told him that I was pretty sure. I had been trained to see even when taking evasive action. He sent a detective over to check out the tower. He came back a few minutes later with a confirmation that somebody had been up there. They were going to process it for fingerprints, DNA, etc. There was not a shell casing. That was to be expected. He asked me if I had any idea why anybody would want to take a shot at me and I told him, "No! In fact, I don't really know anybody in this town. I came into town for the funeral of Dr. Lucas. Prior to that, I had been here for a week each year for the past twenty years or so, but I didn't get to know any of the locals. As far as I know, I don't have any enemies here."

"Are you planning on staying?" he asked.

"Well, it looks like I'll be here at least part of the time. Dr. Lucas gave the church and house to me. He wants me to continue what he started."

He grinned, "I hope you live long enough to do it! I'm member of your church, by the way."

"I am so pleased to meet you even though I believe we could have met without all the fireworks," I responded.

He chuckled out loud at that. "I'm going to leave an officer here for the rest of the day and the evening. You be careful, please."

"Thanks, Sergeant Cooper. I will do my best," I told him.

After the police left, I got into the Caddy that Doc Lucas had left me and decided to take a drive rather than a walk to try to clear my head. As I turned the corner beside the Catholic Church, I saw Steve Lucas coming out of the church. He was walking with a tall priest and seemed to be in an animated conversation with him. I didn't give it much thought. Steve had gone high school here and done his undergraduate work here as well. It didn't seem like a big deal at the time.

When I got back to Stone House, I put the car in the garage and went into the house through the garage. I was now more conscious of my movements. I was starting to think like a soldier again. I didn't want that to happen. Those were not good days. I was too old for this; for goodness sake, I was past sixty. This was no time to start getting shot at. This was the time to be thinking about retirement, and here I was embroiled in something that I did not understand at all. Why would anybody want me dead? Maybe it was just a warning, but I knew better. That shot had been aimed for my head. Whoever was behind this wanted me dead. This just did not make any sense. Could it be because of something that Doc had left for me? That made some sense, but not much. I just couldn't think of anything that I had done, said, or even thought that might get me killed. Life was suddenly very confusing. I wondered what kind of rollercoaster ride God was taking me on. I really knew that God never does or allows anything without a purpose. Well, if he was telling me to be careful, I got the message. Starting tomorrow, I was going to have to try to figure out what was going on and why. I had a suspicion that this could be a long road before I got to the bottom of this.

I was hungry. I went to the kitchen and grabbed a salad and went to the library to eat it. When I opened the door to my suite, I was shocked. It had been completely torn apart. My clothes were everywhere, my books were torn apart, the bed and all of the furniture were all torn up. I called 911 for the second time that day.

By the time the police were done, it was eleven o'clock and my salad had long since wilted. I gave up on dinner and went to bed. As I was lying in bed before falling asleep, my mind was casting about for some explanation to what had happened. Who would want me dead? Who went through my stuff and what were they looking for? I hope they found it so they'll leave me alone. All grousing aside, I really need some answers.

CHAPTER 5

I awakened to the sound of thunder and then another flash of lightning. It was storming outside. I rolled over and tried to get comfortable, but I could not sleep. I got up and padded into the library with my slippers making a soft sound on the marble floor. I turned on the light on the desk and sat there doing nothing for a few minutes. Why had Doc put me in this spot? With Doc it was about the work, not about the workman. Of that I was sure. No matter what Danny had said about Doc loving me, there was more to it. Doc loved a lot of people and respected many of them. There was more to this than love and respect. It had to be about the work. Doc was always about the work. What was it that he wanted me to do? Once again, there were more questions than answers. The toughest part for me was that I didn't even know where to start. There was not a hint of what was in Doc's mind when he turned this place and his work over to me. There was the one book that I had found, but a dozen people could have finished the book better than I could. More than that, really. There were a dozen that I could think of off the top of my head. I was going to start by looking at the boxes that Bill and I had put in the safe yesterday afternoon. It seemed like a week ago.

I took the key from around my neck and opened the safe, putting the key back around my neck. There were six boxes. One of them was labeled "Theology." That would be for another time. The second one was labeled "UFOs." I was in no mood for that at this hour of the morning/night. The third box was labeled "History of Western Civilization." That would bear some study, but not now. The fourth box was labeled "Aztecs/Mayans." That looked interesting. Maybe I'd get into this box after I checked out what was in the others. The fifth box was labeled "chicken scratching of Doc Lucas." That caught my eye, but what really caught my eye was the fact that the sixth box was not labeled. Doc was the most organized man that I knew. He labeled everything so that he could find it when he wanted it. Everything was in a file somewhere, and he could put his hand on it anytime that he wanted it. The papers always went right back into the proper place after use too. He was very careful, so it was notable that he had not labeled this last box. I put the other boxes back into the safe and carried the unmarked box over to one of the work tables. I sat it down and pulled the top off.

Inside the box were several journals which were dated. I picked up the first one and opened it. It was dated several years before right after one of our annual meetings. The date was January 29, 2009. This was the note he had written:

> Jack and I discussed last days' prophecies during
> out last meeting. It was a very intriguing discussion.
> We talked about the second coming on which we
> do not agree. We talked about the mark of the beast
> on which hardly anybody agrees. We discussed
> the man of sin, the false prophet, and many other

aspects of end times that have been discussed until probably every possibility has been mentioned. We're just not sure which ones are true. It's an interesting problem. It really became interesting when we started discussing Matthew chapter 24. We were talking about verse 24: "For false Christs and false prophets will rise and show great signs and wonders to deceive, if possible, even the elect." Jack offered a thought that I originally rejected outright. His thought was if it were possible to clone Jesus from DNA on the shroud of Turin they could actually bring a false Christ in the cloned body of the real Christ. My initial reaction was that it was not possible; God would not allow it. But what if it were possible? What would that mean? With the things that modern medicine can do they might find in the DNA of the blood of Jesus. All of that was conjecture as well. Then the discussion started to get both interesting and a bit frightening. Jack said, I remember his words clearly, "If they could clone one, they could clone a hundred or a thousand. The Catholic Church has the shroud and they have thousands of nuns who are potential surrogate mothers to these clones. All they would need is the technology. Could it be?" We stared at each other for several long moments then Jack dropped the bombshell of the night: "That would be the ultimate abomination that brings desolation if Satan were to inhabit the very fleshly sanctuary that had been the habitation of God on earth and proclaims himself to be God. Maybe we're looking in the wrong direction for this abomination. Maybe the temple that is to be rebuilt is not on temple mount at all." We could hardly breathe after that. We were both excited at the possibilities of a new direction of thought and somewhat overwhelmed at the raw evil of the potential plot. We decided that it was time to hit the sack. We would need clearer heads to discuss this further.

I remembered that conversation well. The next morning, though, neither of us brought it up again. I remembered saying those things to Doc and he just looked at me and grunted. I thought that he thought that I had lost my marbles. We never discussed it again. From the note in his journal, he didn't think I was nuts. In fact, from the looks of the other journals in the box, he may have carried on an investigation into the idea. There were a dozen journals in the box. That was somewhat gratifying to me. I put the box back into the safe and locked it. It was about four thirty in the morning and I was sleepy again, so I decided to try to sleep for a while longer.

When I awakened again, it was full daylight. I got up, made coffee, and jumped into the shower. When I was out of the shower, the coffee was ready and I had my first sip of the day. It was good. I looked at the clock and it was 9:00 a.m. I walked into Jennifer's office and told her that I would be gone next week. I had a fishing trip planned with an old friend. I asked her to set up a meeting with the church board for the week after next. Everything was to continue as it had before until then. I would plan on speaking for the first time as senior pastor on the first Sunday morning of the month. She smiled and said, "That's what Dr. Lucas always did."

I replied, "I didn't know, but I'm glad. There is no need to upset a smooth routine. Thanks for everything."

I went to the library and called the travel agency. Once again, I found that a ticket had already been paid in advance. I booked the flight for tomorrow and walked over the Stone Church. It was quiet in there. I spoke briefly with Larry Smith, the associate pastor who did most of the preaching. I had known him for a number of years. He asked me if I was going to make any changes. My response was, "Why try to fix something that isn't broken? We will maintain the schedule and ministries as they are for the time being. We will deal with problems that arise. Changing things just to make changes is not a good approach to management. I say forward with no detours or delays."

He replied, "No wonder Doc Lucas picked you to lead. You sound just like him." I told him that I would be gone for a week or more as I had a fishing trip planned. We made plans to get together for a meeting when I got back from my fishing trip.

I had a brainstorm when I got back to the library. I made a sudden, impulsive decision to move the journals in the sixth box to a safe deposit box before leaving town. I thought that I would take one of them with me. I opened the safe and took the journals out of the box and placed them in my briefcase. I then put the empty box back in the safe and left for the bank. I decided to use a bank other than the one that the church used. I'm not really sure why I did that, but I did. I drove across town to the First State Bank and went inside. I filled out the paperwork and paid for the box a year in advance. Setting the first journal aside, I started to load the others into the safe deposit box. In impulse, I grabbed the second one too, and then loaded the others into the box, closed it up, and left the bank. As an afterthought, almost, I put the key to the safe deposit box on the chain around my neck with the key to the safe in the library. I went back to Stone House and packed and drove to the airport. I called Jennifer and asked them to pick up my car at the airport after telling her where Doc kept the spare keys. I apologized for not planning better and having one of them drive me to the airport. She said they didn't mind. One of their favorite restaurants was over on that side of town, so they could use it as an excuse to go out to eat.

I checked in, checked my bags, and sat down to wait for the flight. Then for some reason I was really sleepy, wrapped the strap of my carry-on around my wrist and dozed off. When I was a kid, we used to noddle for cat fish. That was a way of catching them up under the banks of the river and reaching in and grabbing them with our bare hands. It was a bit crazy, but we thought it was fun. I was dreaming that I had a hold of a big catfish and it was fighting and pulling on my right arm. I woke up and a man had his foot tangled inside the strap of my carry-on. He was trying to pull loose, and in the process pull the carry-on away from me. My right hand had been down at my side, and he apparently didn't notice that the strap was wrapped around my wrist. I jumped up and grabbed him, sat him down in the seat next to mine, and pulled his foot out of my carry-on. Then I stood over him so that he could not walk away and demanded of him, "What do you think you're doing?"

His response was in very broken English, "I very sorry, sir! Accident!" The airport police were coming over by that time and asked what was going on. I told them that the guy tried to steal my carry-on bag. He kept babbling about it being an accident, but it looked like he tried to kick my bag away while I was dozing. He would have gotten away with it, if I had not wrapped the strap around my wrist. I mean, I don't want to sound paranoid, but this was really getting weird! My stuff back at Stone House had been searched, I had been shot at, and now this. What is going on?

Airport security asked me if I wanted to press charges. I told them that I was asleep, so if there were no other witnesses, there would be no proof of what happened. I was awakened by this guy with his foot tangled up in the strap of the carry-on. I didn't see what led up to it. They said that they had canvassed for witnesses and nobody saw what happened. They only responded to the ruckus. I told them that there would be no point in pressing charges, so they let him go. He was complaining that he had already missed his flight. I just ignored him and got ready to board the flight to Houston.

On the flight, I pulled Doc's first journal out and started reading the second entry.

February 15, 2009

I have decided that it is time to give a serious study to the ideas that Jack and I discussed back in the last week of December. As outrageous as it appears, there's enough substance to it to merit a good review. How thorough we get depends on what is uncovered as we proceed.

First of all, I am going to give a careful study to whether or not it is even possible to clone humans. It is legal in the USA. It seems curious that the USA would outlaw something that could not possibly be done. Secondly, we need to study the shroud of Turin to see if there is, was, or possibly could be viable DNA on it from which an attempt could be made to clone. Thirdly, it is very important to study the scriptural passages related to the "beast/antichrist" to see if it would be a scripturally supported position that could move from a postulate into the level of a working theory.

We will, no doubt, find numerous other angles as we work through this. Most of the areas of study will fit under these three larger studies. We reserve the right to change the direction of the study as facts are uncovered. At this time, we can't really say that we are studying with any other intent except to validate or debunk that idea. In simple words, can it be? Is it possible? Once we have answered that question, we will either pursue the study and follow the facts or close it out.

February 27, 2009

After considerable research on the subject of cloning, it has become clear that some cloning of humans has been attempted. The successes are hard to ascertain because most of the work is done under careful security and all of it outside of the United States. The results are not reported in journals that can be accessed by the average person. It seems fairly certain that human cloning is thought to be possible. Some are certain that it has already been done successfully. The technology and results are heavily guarded, but that alone indicates that something is going on. Why guard experiments that are going nowhere?

It has been somewhat of a mystery that the antichrist is called "the beast" rather than a man. The pronouns used in Scripture, however, are the masculine personal pronouns, which would seem to indicate that he has the form of a man, but is not considered human by God. Under the inspiration of the Holy Spirit, the apostle John refers to the antichrist as "the beast" rather than a man. The same passages, however, also use the masculine personal pronouns. I wonder why.

The reason that this raises a question is that nothing in Scripture is accidental. God did not misspeak. What is it about the antichrist that is inhuman or nonhuman or whatever? One possible theory is that it is because of the nature of the antichrist; because he is so cruel that it is inhuman. Although possible, that seems weak. In the Bible, angels are called angels, demons are called demons, men are called men. The antichrist is not called any of these. Neither is he called God, although he tries to make that claim himself. He is called "the beast." Even in Revelation chapter 13 verse 18 the language is specific: "Here is wisdom. Let him who has understanding calculate the number of the beast, for it is the number of a man: His number is 666." The verse clearly says that although the number is the number of a man, it does not call the antichrist a man, it calls him "the beast." That has to be significant.

Another possible theory is that he comes up out of the bottomless pit and that his origin is uncertain. That doesn't hold simply because nothing is a mystery to God. Another possibility is that the antichrist will be a clone of a person who has lived and died. There is a fairly prominent view that a human clone may not have a soul. The reasoning behind this is that a person's soul is related to the spirit or life that is in him. Some believe that because when we die, our spirit returns to God who gave it. If that is true, by cloning a human, we would be acting in opposition to God's natural plan for life and death. Unless God would release the original spirit back into a cloned human, he would be a being without a soul. That by definition would be a beast, as any other animal on the planet. It is frightening to think this could happen, but it is not outside the realm of possibility.

If the antichrist is a clone of someone who has died, who could it be? Revelation 17:10 and 11 have a curious tone in this regard: "There are also seven kings. Five have fallen, one is, and the other has not yet come. And when he comes, he must continue a short time. The beast that was, and is not, is himself also the eighth, as is of the seven, and is going to perdition." This is a curious description because the language used *could* be construed to support the idea of a clone. It is also noteworthy that the beast was cast alive into the lake of fire, per Revelation 19:20. This was done without the benefit of judgment, which also lends credence to the notion that the beast is not human, but something else.

That was the end of the entry, and by now my head was spinning again. These were some of the ideas that Doc and I had discussed, but he had never indicated that he was giving it any serious thought. It looked like he was trying to make the case. He sometimes would take a seemingly preposterous idea and start defending it until it became indefensible. It was one of his methods of study. He felt that dismissing a preposterous idea because it was preposterous, was intellectually dishonest. That is how he came to believe that there could be life on other planets. There was no scriptural reason to be against it. Historically, it seemed feasible. He didn't go so far as to say that he believed that there was life on other planets. He just admitted that it was possible. He felt that it would explain some things that were otherwise very hard to explain. It was a method that I recognized, and he was using it in his study of the idea that the beast of Daniel and Revelation was a clone of a long dead person brought back and possessed by Satan to raise himself up as God. I needed to read the rest of these journals, but my plane was starting its decent into Houston so it would have to wait.

After landing, I met my friend Jerry who was picking me up at the baggage claim area. We grabbed my bags and headed for home. It was about two thirty and I hadn't had lunch, so we stopped at my favorite place for fajitas and had a late lunch. Jerry dropped me off at my house at about four in the afternoon. I went through my mail throwing most of it in the trash. There were some letters that I would need to read and some bills that needed paying. That I could do tomorrow. I peeled off my clothes and put a swimsuit on and jumped into my backyard pool. The water was quite warm, but still felt refreshing. I needed some exercise, so I did about a half hour of laps up and down the length of the pool varying my stroke. Then I just floated in the water and enjoyed the warm Texas sunshine. It felt good to be home. There wasn't much in the refrigerator for dinner, so I decided to go out. I'd pick up a few things tomorrow, but not too much as I'd be leaving again early next week. I walked out into my front yard and saw my neighbor lady, Esmeralda. She was a Hispanic lady. She told me that she had seen several people drive up to my house and knock on the door. I told her that nobody had left a card or anything like that. After talking with her, I decided that I had better keep Doc Lucas's journals in my safe when I wasn't reading them. I went back into the house and put the journals in the safe. This was a combination safe, so I didn't need a key. I was feeling hungry after swimming and looked at my watch; it was about seven thirty-five and time for dinner.

I went to a local cafeteria that was a few blocks from my house. There I could get some baked fish. After fajitas for lunch, it was important to eat healthy. I have a tendency to gain weight, so I have to be very careful about what I eat. I ordered a dinner salad with vinegar and oil, baked salmon, and green beans. I did not pick up any bread or dessert. It was a small victory, but I congratulated myself just the same. After dinner, I drove home and settled down to watch a little TV. I fell asleep watching TV, and when I woke up all of the lights were off in the house. I sat there without moving, but something had awakened me. I had heard something. After a moment, I realized that I had heard somebody at the back door. They were trying to open it. I got up without turning on any lights and slipped quietly toward the back door. There in the moonlight I could see a man trying to open the door. I could plainly see his face, and to my surprise, it was the guy that had tried to steal my bag at the airport. Now that was really strange. I stayed in the shadows and waited while the man patiently picked the lock on my back door. As he stepped into the house, my military training took over. I had him on the floor with my knee in his back so quickly that he didn't know what hit him. I took off the belt from my robe and tied his hands behind his back and then reached over and turned on the light. I'm not sure which of us was more surprised. I had not expected to see him again, and he thought that I was asleep. I got some rope and quickly secured his hands better and then searched him. I found a 9mm Glock and two knives on him. I then sat him on a chair and just looked at him. I asked him, "What in the world are you doing in my house?" He tried the broken English trick on me again, but I told him, "Don't play with me, buddy. You are in some serious trouble. It would be in your best interest to level with me!"

He said, "You have no idea what you are talking about. The people that sent me are very serious. If I tell you what is going on, I'm a dead man."

I responded, "I have already figured out that it has something to do with Doc Lucas's research. I just don't know what yet. I will figure it out, though."

He responded, "Do yourself a favor and just burn the journals. You don't need the grief that they are going to bring you."

I decided to search him again. The first time through I was just looking for weapons. I decided to look at his ID too. Pulling out his wallet, I found that his name was Julio Gonzalez, if that was in fact his real name. He had car keys, so I figured that he must have driven. I tied him securely to the chair and then went outside with his car keys. Hitting the panic button on the key ring soon pinpointed which car it was. I opened the car and found his briefcase and his luggage. He wasn't going to need them in jail, so I took them into the house. When I went back into the house, I could hear him trying to free himself from the chair, but I have restrained a few people in my lifetime. He wasn't going anywhere. When I walked back into the kitchen where he was tied, he had a bit of a grouch on. "Where did you learn to tie these knots?" he grumbled.

I responded, "Oh, I just picked them up along the way. Pretty good knots, aren't they?"

"They're really good, although I hate to admit it," he said.

"Now I'm going to find out who you really are," I said and started searching through his briefcase.

He was really tense as I started looking through his papers. He said, "Those are private! You have no right to look through them!"

I chuckled at that and told him, "You should have thought about that before you broke into my house. Last I knew, that too is private. The difference is that there is no law against me searching your luggage and briefcase since I'm not a cop. I'm going to find out what you are up to and, if possible, find out for whom you are working." Then he became really angry. He started speaking to me in a language that I didn't understand, and I don't think he was giving me his mother's fried chicken recipe.

At the bottom of his briefcase, I found it. It was an Italian passport and diplomatic credentials from the Vatican. I sat back and we just stared at each other for a full minute or maybe more. "Do you want to tell me about it?" I asked him.

He sighed and said, "I will tell you what I can without endangering my life."

"I'm okay with that," I responded.

He started, "Your friend, Dr. Lucas, has been on our radar for about a year and a half. We picked up the subject of several of his Internet searches and started to pay attention to what he was paying attention to."

"You can do that?" I asked him.

"We have first class intelligence gathering people working for us and with us," he responded. "We have a file on you too. Your friendship with Dr. Lucas and your natural inquisitiveness makes you a person to whom we would pay attention."

"Wow! That is both bizarre and a bit scary!" I responded.

He smiled and said, "We had hoped to scare Dr. Lucas away from the nature of his studies, but found that he really didn't scare very easily."

That made me laugh right out loud. The thought of Doc being scared of anything was ludicrous. I told him, "He was a chaplain with a marine division during World War II. He saw lots of action, and the man was as fearless as any that I have ever known. Especially at his age, you weren't going to scare him. He knew that he wasn't going to live long anyway. Truth was his true passion in the last few years of his life. Once he got the scent, he was like a hound on the trail."

He agreed, "That he was. He just would not stop. How about you? Are you going to be like him and follow this out?"

My response was, "To be quite honest, I don't know. I haven't had a chance to read through them yet. I should warn you, though. I have had some pretty serious military training. You guys have broken into my room at Stone House, shot at me, tried to steal my bag at the airport, and broken into my house. I feel like taking the gloves off and start playing your game. Trust me, you would rather I didn't do that. Frankly, I am way better at it than you are. Now, I'm going to call the police."

He sighed and said, "For what it's worth, that shot was not intended to hit you, just to scare you."

I looked him right in the eye and said in a very soft and very angry voice, "You, sir, are a liar." Then I called the police.

When the police arrived, Julio kept trying to tell them that he had diplomatic immunity. They asked him to show them some proof of such. He was searching through his bag trying to find his diplomatic ID from the Vatican. He was showing some desperation. That amused me a little. I grinned and glanced toward my incinerator, which had made short work of his documents. I was especially glad that I had wiped down his bag after handling it. They wouldn't find any evidence that I had touched it. That was also true of the car. I didn't expect that destroying the diplomatic documents would stop him, but I hoped that it would slow him down for a couple of days. Julio gave me a dirty look when they walked him out in handcuffs. That really made me smile.

CHAPTER 6

When the police took Julio Gonzales away, I had very little hope that he would actually go to trial. It was almost certain that his first phone call would be to his superiors who would have him out of there almost before he sat down in the holding cell. The chances that he would actually be there for trial were not great. I certainly would not bet on it. But at least he had enlightened me some regarding the strange things that had been happening. Doc Lucas must have really hit on something that somebody did not want revealed. Julio didn't tell me what it was that had his superiors so worried. I was going to have to figure that out on my own. That meant reading Doc's notes in great detail. Doc had found something that he thought needed to be investigated that somebody else did not want revealed. I wanted to really try to think it through, but I was too sleepy. I went to bed. It had been a long day.

I was up early in the morning. After some quiet time, I jumped into the pool and swam for about a half hour. I had really missed my pool while up north. Then I took a quick shower and scrambled some eggs for breakfast. While I was eating it occurred to me that I should have the locks changed on the house. It was apparent that the locks that I had on the doors were not very secure. I should also consider getting a security system put in. I made a couple of calls to get those projects in motion and then went in to check e-mail, review correspondence, and pay some bills. By ten o'clock, those projects were finished.

I decided to run to the grocery store and pick up a few things for the next few days. While I was in the store, my cell phone rang. It was the locksmith that I had called. He had some recommendations, and we discussed them. He asked when he could get to work, and I told him that I would be home all afternoon. He said he would be there at around one thirty. I finished my shopping and was getting ready to drive home when I felt the sudden craving for another cup of coffee. There was a coffee shop in the same complex with the grocery store, so I headed over there. I had been there a few times, so the young man behind the counter recognized me. "Hi, Jack!" he chirped.

"Hi, Billy," I responded. "I'll just have my usual." My thing is strong, black coffee. I like the fancy stuff, okay, but what I really want is just strong, black coffee. I don't like it bitter, but I do like it strong. He handed me my coffee, and I paid for it and grabbed a *Houston Chronicle* that somebody had left behind and sat down to enjoy my coffee.

As I browsed the paper, I noted that city hall and the Houston Police Department were squabbling over money. Now there's a shock. There was other uninteresting "news." On the religion page, I saw an article on the shroud of Turin. That thing had always fascinated me. There was so much legend and so much mystery about it. This article was another on the authenticity of it. The conclusion of this article was that they could not confirm that it was authentic, but could not rule it out either. Nothing had really changed since the last time somebody tried to figure out where it came from and how it was created. I have my opinion, but it's just that. I am not a scientist. I'm a pretty good historical researcher, but not a scientist. With me it's more of a hobby than a profession. One of the luxuries that a hobbyist enjoys is that we don't feel so compelled to find hard answers. We are often satisfied that we have gained more knowledge for ourselves. Speaking only for myself, I get very excited when I find another piece or two of the puzzle. Especially when I am sure that it fits. That is exciting!

I flipped over to the sports page. The Astros were floundering again. It seemed perpetual. I remembered the great 2005 season and wished for those days again. Being a realist, however, I turned the pages until I found the comics. Now there is real life! I browsed the comics. There was nothing very funny. I did smile at "Family Circle," but it was weak. I finished my coffee, and it was time to move on.

At home, I made a couple of decisions. I wanted to take Doc's journals with me, but did not want to expose them to theft while I was fishing. It made sense to scan the journals onto a computer disc and carry them that way. I did that and noted that I had about an hour before the locksmith arrived, so I quickly ran up to the bank, which was just a few blocks away, and placed the original journals in my safe deposit box. They would be safe there. I drove back home and made a sandwich, which I finished just a few minutes before the doorbell rang. It was the locksmith. We discussed the security of my home, and he went to work changing the locks.

They were designed so that they could not be opened without a key from the outside or the inside. If somebody broke in, they would have to break back out. They weren't going to use any of the doors without breaking them down. A new security system would take care of that. The security people would come in the morning to install a very comprehensive security system. My home would not be impregnable, but nobody could get in without raising a ruckus. That was about the best I could do without a pit bull or armed guards.

When the locksmith was finished, I sat down at my computer and slipped the disc of Doc's journals into the drive. I picked up where I had left off. This one was dated March 10, 2009. Doc said:

> Since everybody and his brother have tried to figure out who the antichrist is using numerology and various systems assigning letters numerical value, I am not going to even attempt to address the number 666 in that manner. Nearly everything that could be said on that subject has been said without any conclusive results. I want to look at it from a different point of view. I noted in my research that in cloning Dolly the sheep, there were around 274 unsuccessful attempts before a successful clone was achieved. Let's assume that human cloning would be much more complicated than animal cloning. The number of a man, 666, could be the number assigned after 665 failures to achieve a successful clone.
>
> There is the issue of the viability of cells after 2000 years. It should be kept in mind, however, that the

DNA on the shroud might still be viable, if it is indeed the DNA of Jesus. There are a couple of possibilities that should be addressed regarding this. One is the fact that some unknown process occurred to imprint the image on the shroud of Turin. We don't know what that was, but it may have preserved the viability of the DNA along with the image. We don't know, but should not discount, the possibility. The second issue is the fact that although very man of very man, Christ was also very God of very God. His DNA was not normal human DNA. It could not have been. The potential for viable DNA in this case is better than for any other man that lived and died. I'm not saying that it is, in fact, viable. I could not know; it just is not wise to totally discount the possibility.

There is also the question of whether or not God would allow this to happen. That is a good question. This question is side by side with other questions that are every bit as difficult such as, "Why did God allow Adam to sin in the first place?" Allowing the cloned flesh of Jesus to be used by the antichrist as his earthly temple would be somewhat comparable to God allowing Adam to sin and thereby bringing sin and sinfulness upon all of us. At least it is not completely out of the realm of possibility. Recalling how God allowed sin to abound, knowing that grace would much more abound, causes one to think that

God may allow things that we would never permit, because he has the purposes and plans that we could not begin to comprehend. The deception of the antichrist would be enhanced by inhabiting the cloned flesh of Jesus. It is not as though Satan would be possessing the body of Jesus. He was raised bodily from the grave. He ascended bodily to the Father, is seated bodily at the right hand of the Majesty on high, and he will return bodily to this earth to reign. This would be another counterfeit messiah manufactured by the evil genius of this world. This is one of the most intriguing concepts that has come across my desk in many years.

Another possible explanation for the number 666 came from a book I read recently. The idea of this author was that the antichrist is coming out of the European Economic Union. The EEU is comprised, generally, of the countries that made up the Roman Empire. There have been several attempts to revive the Roman Empire over the centuries. One notable example is Adolf Hitler and his Third Reich. To date, it has never been successful. It seems that the EEU is having more success than their predecessors. They have a common currency and a common purpose. They also have their own government in Brussels, Belgium. In their assembly hall there are around 750 seats, all of which have not been assigned. One of the unassigned seats is the one bearing the number 666. The author of this book postulated that the person assigned the seat number 666 would ultimately become the antichrist.

This theory is not without merit. It has connections that are well-founded in prophetic utterance. We could note that these theories do not need to be exclusive. It could be one or the other, both, or a combination of the two. There also remains the possibility that none of our theories are correct.

When I finished reading this entry, I noticed that it was just five in the afternoon. I turned the TV on to watch *The Five* on Fox News. That was one of my favorite news and commentary shows. They were discussing the economy, which seemed like a daily topic of conversation on and off TV news. I was feeling sleepy and felt myself dozing.

When I woke up it was six thirty and I was hungry. I got up to fix something to eat and noticed that I had a message on my phone. It was the security company. They were confirming that they would be there tomorrow morning at nine and expected to be there all morning and maybe part of the afternoon. That was fine with me. The sooner the better, as far as I was concerned. I fixed a salad and put some tuna in it. It wasn't my favorite dinner, but I try sometimes to eat healthy. My concession to pleasure eating was some good French bread that I had picked up at the store this morning. While I was eating I pondered what I should do with my place in Houston. It really wasn't necessary to sell it. It was paid for, so there was no expense except of upkeep and taxes. The neighbor kid would take care of the lawn and pool. That cost me about $150.00 per month, which included the chemicals. I had thought about listing the place, but really didn't want to part with it. The market wasn't strong. I wouldn't lose money on it because I had bought well and done some work on the place. By the time my salad was gone, I had decided to hold onto the place for a while. It made sense to have a warm place to run when the winters up north began their vengeful attacks on the poor inhabitants of the land. Until something significant changed, I was going to keep it.

After eating and making a decision about the house, I called my fishing partner in Michigan and told him that I would be there by the weekend. We would plan on fishing whatever days we could next week. He said that the weather forecast looked favorable for most of the week. He also told me that the river wasn't high and, as long as there was minimal rain, we should have no trouble floating the Muskegon River. There is nothing in this world quite like floating the river. It is so quiet out there. You don't hear cars and all the noises of civilization. The sounds out there are the sounds of nature. Even when the world is quiet, it isn't silent. There are sounds that we don't hear until we get away from the noises that we make. That's what floating the river does. Mike and I have some great conversations, but it doesn't scare us to have silence between us. We can sit in the boat together and enjoy the sounds around us without saying a word. That is a rare friendship. It's one that I value.

After talking with Mike, I decided to go for a walk. I could walk down to the north end of the subdivision and back to make just over a mile. I started out and almost immediately ran into an older neighbor who had served with John F. Kennedy during

WWII. He never got tired of telling and retelling his stories. He didn't think much of JFK as a naval officer, but he liked him as president. This I knew from many chats over the years. Ollie was not feeling very well this evening, so he didn't feel like talking. I couldn't help but think that he wouldn't be around much longer. He was quite feeble. That didn't stop him from getting out in his lawn and trying to scare every weed into next month, though. I'd hate to be a weed trying to make a living in his yard. I had seen him down on his hands and knees digging weeds out of his yard. The old man was relentless, I'll say that much for him.

When I got home after my walk, I went out into the garage to begin getting my stuff together for the fishing trip. I really didn't need to do much. Mostly, I needed to clean and oil my reels and change the line. I try to change the line on them at the very least once a year. Keeping good strong line on the reels can be the difference between landing or losing a big fish. I put four- and six-pound test line on my two light reels that I like to use for river fishing. I then put twelve-pound line on my heavier reel that I like to use for pike fishing. We might get a chance to go over to Pere Marquette Lake in Ludington and do some pike fishing. You never know. I made sure that my favorite rods were in the rod carrier and then went in to shower and go to bed. I was tired.

I slept a bit late the next morning. My eyes opened at 7:39. The sun was already up, and the sounds of the city were beginning. I put on my shorts and running shoes and headed out for a morning jog. I don't run hard anymore. I jogged a couple of miles in about twenty minutes. When I got back to the house, I put the coffee pot on and took a quick shower. I made a fruit bowl for breakfast. It consisted of some strawberries, half a banana, grapes, cheese, and peanuts. I mixed a small container of low fat cherry yogurt into the concoction, added a few cheerios, and headed down the hallway with my breakfast and coffee in hand. I sat down in my office and decided to enjoy some quiet time while I ate my breakfast. I was lost in meditation when the doorbell rang. The security company technician had arrived to install my new security system.

While the security system was being installed, I made a few phone calls, paid some bills, and checked e-mail. I had an e-mail from Jennifer wondering when I would be back at Stone House. I sent her back a reply indicating that it would be about two weeks. I suggested that she could set a staff meeting for Wednesday morning two weeks out. If that was inconvenient, she was to schedule it when it would be convenient. I told her that I thought nine in the morning would work and that everyone should block out the morning. Hopefully it would not take that long, but I could. I also told her that I would expect written and verbal reports from each department and would like to see the budget.

I then went to the kitchen to grab another cup of coffee. The tech was finished installing the security system and wanted to show me how it worked. I offered him a cup of coffee, and he accepted. While we were sipping our coffee, he walked me through the nuts and bolts of using the security system. He showed me how to set and change the code. Once we had gone over the use of the system, he tested it to make sure that it called to the monitoring center. After a few more pleasantries, he left. Hopefully, the new locks and the security system would prevent any further break-in incidents.

CHAPTER 7

There were a few days before I needed to leave for my fishing trip. Even if I drove, I wouldn't need to leave until Friday or Saturday. I decided that I wanted to do some research at the University of Texas Medical School in Galveston before leaving. I drove to Galveston arriving at around two thirty in the afternoon. The library had a sign indicating that it would close at ten in the evening. That was more than enough time for today. I requested assistance and asked for the latest articles on cloning. It seemed like I was going to need to study the subject and especially the recent developments in the field.

I pulled several journals and reference sources and started reading and taking notes. There were numerous articles describing the cloning of animals. It was quite common by this time. The material on the cloning of humans was shrouded in secrecy. It was hard to find any reports that actually admitted the cloning of human beings. Even in the countries where it is not prohibited, there were not clear reports that admitted success. The technology was discussed up to a point, and the theories were bandied about. There were allusions to tests, but no photos of a cloned human and no claims of success. On the other hand, the reports did not discuss failures either. It seemed like a conspiracy of silence. The history of cloning was discussed going back to the Nazi experiments going back to WWII. The reports on the cloning of animals was discussed in detail, but beyond that point, they became murky and nonspecific.

I did find a research facility in Mexico that was run by a private corporation and apparently funded by huge research grants from some of the large tech companies. It looked like there were hundreds of millions of dollars in grants coming in. The description of their work is simply stated as genetic research. There was really nothing else of substance stated. Their website encouraged contributions and offered to take donations via VISA, MasterCard, etc. They were quite enterprising in that regard. While trying to learn specifics of their work prior to making a donation (which I had no intention of doing), I was booted out of the site. It seemed that they were very willing to take my money, but didn't want me asking questions. The name of the company is the Sunrise Corporation. They were incorporated in Delaware, but their offices there just showed a street address with no phone number. I tried to get a phone number via directory assistance using the name and address of the corporation. There was no phone listed in the USA.

I did read several reports where animals that had been considered extinct had been successfully cloned. They did not go into detail as to how they found viable cells to use in the process. One of the articles "theorized" that by replacing the nucleus of a viable cell with the DNA of an unviable cell and then passing a low voltage electrical current through it, viability could be restored. Although none of the articles "claimed" that this process had been successful, it is reasonable to presume that it has been attempted. Minus a report indicating that it was a failure, it is at least reasonable to conclude that there has been some success using this method.

I looked at my watch and noted that it was 6:30 p.m. My head ached and my sit-down wanted to stand up awhile. I went to the copy area and made copies of the articles that I had found interesting and then headed out. On the way home, I stopped at Blackbeard's for one of their very excellent hamburgers. I shouldn't have, but I did. It was great.

Arriving home, I checked phone messages and e-mail. There were no phone messages that required immediate attention, for which I was thankful. There was an e-mail from Jennifer confirming the meeting with the staff of Stone Church as I had requested. I put on my swimming trunks and swam for about forty-five minutes. Sitting all afternoon in the library had built up some unused physical energy. By the time I was done swimming, that was gone and I felt relaxed and ready to wind down for the night.

I hit the sack at around eleven fifteen and was watching the late news while preparing to doze. I was too sleepy to watch the news, so I turned off the TV and the light and settled down to sleep. I was in that nebulous area between being awake and asleep while really being all the way in either camp when the thought occurred to me that I should make a quick trip to Mexico to see what I could find out about the Sunrise Corporation. I jumped out of bed and ran to my office, which was a converted bedroom, and quickly booked a flight to Monterrey, Mexico, for the next day at around noon. The return flight would be the next afternoon at four forty-five. Then I went to bed and went to sleep.

I was up right at the crack of dawn the next morning. There were just a few things that I needed to do before leaving for Mexico. I wanted to be sure that the kid next door would be mowing the lawn and cleaning the pool before the end of the week, and I wanted to talk to him about long-term maintenance, since I would be spending most of my time in West Virginia for the foreseeable future. I called him at around eight in the morning. He said he'd be right over and was there almost before I could walk to the door. Zeke, his name was Ezekiel, was a sophomore in high school, so he could for sure take care of my place for the next two years barring any unforeseen circumstances. We agreed on a price for his work and an arrangement where he could bill me for pool supplies, gasoline, weed killer, fertilizer, and the like. We shook on it, and I told him that I would be in and out for the next few weeks. I gave him a key to the garage where everything that he needed was kept.

After Zeke left, I dug around in my junk until I found my passport, packed a bag, and headed to WalMart. I wanted to pick up a few things for my trip. Fortunately for me, the store was on the way to the airport. I picked up a good digital recorder and a high-resolution digital camera. Both were small and easily hidden in a pocket and/or hand. It's not that I wanted to be sneaky, but neither did I want to advertise what I was doing. I then headed for the airport and Old Mexico. Going there was always an adventure.

Arriving in Monterrey, I rented a car and drove to the Sunrise Research facility. I wanted to find a hotel close by there, if possible.

I found a nice hotel about a half mile from the facility and booked a room. I took my stuff up to the room and prepared to go out. While driving past the Sunrise Research building, I had noticed a nice restaurant right across the street from it. It might be a good idea to hang out there awhile and see who came and went. I grabbed a book to read and drove to the restaurant.

When I walked into the restaurant, the coolness of the air conditioning made me wish I would never have to leave. I ordered a salad with grilled chicken and coffee and sat back to observe. I started reading my book, but wasn't really concentrating on it. If I got too engrossed in the book, I would forget my purpose in being there. They brought my salad, and I asked for a bottle of water. I had learned the hard way that one should always drink bottled water in foreign countries. I sat there nibbling on my salad. I saw a mixed group come out of the Sunrise offices and walk across the street to the restaurant where I was seated. They were a noisy bunch and caused quite a stir when they came in. They were talking and laughing. The group was mostly Americans from the sound of it. They were speaking in English. I paid little attention to their conversation until I heard on of them say, "We still don't have a really viable subject." My ears perked up, but their voices dropped down and I could not hear them. Then it seemed like they were arguing and one of them said right out loud, "There's another whole load of them coming in at eight in the morning." I made up my mind that I would be here tomorrow at eight in the morning for sure. They had their break and headed back to work. I finished my salad and sat there sipping my coffee and thinking. I still had more questions than answers. Some things just were not making sense to me.

The next morning, as planned, I was parked in the corner near a window, which gave me a perfect view of the street. I had ordered an omelet and was sipping my coffee while waiting for it. It was just before eight when a bus pulled up in front of Sunrise. The writing on the bus said that it was from Saint Catherine's Convent. I was not really paying a lot of attention until the passengers started coming out of the bus. They were all nuns, and they were all very pregnant. Now, that got my attention. I watched them get off the bus and walk into Sunrise. I counted twenty-four pregnant nuns. This must be the load that I had overheard the employee mention yesterday.

After paying for my breakfast, I wandered over to the bus to see if the driver was around. He was sitting in the air conditioned bus dozing in the driver's seat. I tapped on the door and got his attention. I offered to buy him a cup of coffee, and he willingly accompanied me back to the restaurant. When we sat down, I noticed a man across the restaurant watching us rather closely. I thought that I should keep an eye on him. I did not recognize him, but something about him bothered me.

We chatted for a bit. He told me that he was married and had seven children ranging in age from nineteen to four. His wife stayed home and raised the children. Until he got this job, he had worked two jobs to keep the family going. The job, driving bus, had allowed him to cut back to one job. He did not work for the convent, but for an independent bus company that contracted drivers to them. He told me that there were two convents on the property. The one that was out front was the one where the older nuns stayed. This was also the one that the public could visit. There was another building on the back of the property where the young nuns stayed. Nobody was ever allowed to visit this building. This was also where he would pick up a busload of pregnant nuns every week and bring them to Sunrise. He said that it was a long day, but the pay was good, so he would not complain. I found out that the convent was back in the mountains about a four-hour drive from the city. It was not located close to any large city, but was close to a small village called San Rafael. He also mentioned that there was an orphanage connected with the convent. He thought that the sisters at the convent also ran a school for the children at the orphanage. He noted that in the past few years they had expanded the orphanage a couple of times. He thought that rather curious. He expressed the opinion that they didn't seem to plan very well. "What do you expect," he chuckled, "when it's run by a bunch of women." He grinned a toothy grin, and I couldn't help but chuckle. "A man would think ahead," he said. I asked him if it were possible to visit the orphanage. He did not know, but gave me a phone number where inquiries could be made. He thanked me for the coffee and walked back across the street to his bus.

Several times during our conversation, I noticed that man across the restaurant staring at us. It was almost like he was trying to make out what we were talking about. That was an interesting development.

It was around ten thirty, and I had consumed enough coffee to energize Patton's Army. I drove back to the hotel and made a couple of phone calls. One call went to the number that the bus driver had given me. A very pleasant voice answered on the other end. I told them that I was interested in adopting a child and was told that they had a fairly large orphanage. She told me that we should set up an appointment to visit the orphanage. I asked her if the next morning would be acceptable, and she said that it would be fine. We settled on around ten in the morning for the appointment. She told me to ask for Sister Manuela. After a few more pleasantries, we hung up.

Since the hotel had a pool, I decided to swim for a bit. I needed some exercise, and swimming seemed to help me think. There was nobody in the pool at this time of the day, so I enjoyed nearly an hour of swimming and floating about in the water. I was floating on my back and was almost asleep when I remembered where I had seen the man who had been watching us in the restaurant. He was the priest that I had seen with Steve Lucas back in West Virginia when I drove past the Catholic Church. What was he doing here? I guess he was wondering the same thing about me. It made me wonder if this man had something to do with the attempt on my life. I was going to have to watch myself. That much was clear.

I went back to my room and showered. It had been my plan to skip lunch, but after swimming for nearly an hour, I was really hungry. There was a taco stand just down the street from the hotel. I walked down there and ordered the tacos al pastor loaded. That meant with cilantro, onions, and salsa. They made them with double corn tortillas. Although I usually drink diet soda, I made an exception because regular Coke is perfect with good Mexican food. It was delicious, and I was glad that I had been swimming earlier. I'm not sure it really helped, but it made me feel better about it. By the time my tacos were gone, I was *bien contento*, as they say.

Back in my room, I wondered what my next step should be. I really wanted to go to Sunrise and ask some questions, but that approach would be way too obvious. How was I going to get my questions answered? There had to be a way. I decided to stay away from there for the rest of the day. Maybe there would be something more in Doc's journal.

I set up my laptop and slipped the disc into the drive. After reading several of the entries following the last one that I had read, I found nothing new or significant. It seemed like I was hitting a brick wall. I had my suspicions, but no hard evidence. Maybe my trip to the orphanage would yield more positive results.

CHAPTER 8

I was on the road very early the next morning having secured a map to the orphanage at Saint Catherine's. It was a beautiful morning for a drive in the mountains. I needed to leave by noon to get back to the airport, so I had packed my bags and checked out of the hotel before leaving. The highway wound through the mountains. The peaks towered above me as I drove. I marveled at God's handiwork. The mountains weren't beautiful in the sense of a lush rain forest or a meadow full of waving grass and wild flowers, but they had a majesty that spoke of the greatness of their Creator.

As I neared San Rafael, I saw a sign indicating that Saint Catherine's was to the right. I made the turn and in a few minutes was at the gate. There was a buzzer, which I pushed, and a voice asked me who I was and my business. I explained that I had an appointment at the orphanage, and the gate swung open. There was a security guard that directed me to the correct building.

When I walked in to the orphanage, I saw the office to the right. I walked in and gave my name to the receptionist. Soon a nun came to escort me. We walked through the hallways and courtyards. She told me, "The children are in school. Would you like to observe them?" I told her that I would like that very much. We skirted the edge of a playground with the typical swings, seesaws, etc. Children were running and playing. I noticed that there was a higher ratio of boys to girls than normal. It looked like there were about four or five to one on the playground. I commented to the nun who was escorting me, "I'm surprised to see so many more boys than girls on the playground. Is that the way it is here? Are there really that many more boys than girls?"

She responded in a matter-of-fact way, "Yes, we have a higher population of boys than girls."

"Do you have any idea why that is?" I asked. She just shook her head in a somewhat mystified way. "Hasn't anybody ever noticed that before?" I asked her.

"Nobody has ever asked me that before. Whether or not they noticed, I don't know," she responded.

"Well, it's not typical. Most orphanages that I have visited have a higher female population than male. It just caught my attention. Where do the children come from?" I asked.

"Oh, all over Mexico," she said. She gave me a look that gave me to believe that she did not want to answer any more questions.

Suddenly a little boy around six years old came out of one of the buildings. I smiled at him, but he did not react or respond. A couple of moments later, we were entering the school building and the same little boy came walking out of the building. I looked at him and then quickly looked back across the play area and spotted the little boy that I had seen earlier. They were the same! I asked the nun that was guiding me if they were twins. She quickly said yes, but something in her manner made me curious. I decided to pay attention as we did our walk-through. We went into the school building and observed the children for a bit. Then the nun said that she was going to take me to the administration building where I could get some literature and discuss adoption. As we left the school, she took me by another route that did not pass by the playground. It was a longer route, which seemed strange to me, but I said nothing. When we left the school building, we walked through a lovely garden with flowers and fountains. We passed through a gap in a hedge, and there was a round table with six children sitting together. They were all boys and exactly alike in every way that I could see. They were exactly like the two boys that I had seen at the school except these boys looked to be a couple of years younger. I asked no more questions and acted as though I had not seen them. I had brought my small camera, which I had slipped into my pocket. As we walked past the boys, I slipped the camera out of my pocket and snapped a picture of the boys at the table. I did not hold the camera up to my eye, so I would have to wait until I got out of there to check the quality of the photo. The nun turned to see if I was coming, and I was admiring some beautiful lilies that were growing in the garden. "Do you like flowers?" she asked.

"Yes, my grandfather was a gardener. He always had the most beautiful flowers in his yard and gardens," I responded.

"This is a beautiful place," she said.

"Indeed it is," I replied. We continued to the administration building.

I had a short visit with the administrator in charge of adoptions. She gave me some literature, and it was time for me to head back to Monterrey to catch my flight back to Texas. I really wanted to look at the picture that I had taken, but decided to wait until I was away from the orphanage. I got into my rented car and drove down through the mountains. I dropped the car off at the rental desk and went on to the check in for my flight. I sat down and decided to transfer the photos onto my computer while I was waiting for the flight. I got my computer out and took the chip out of my camera. I transferred the photos and then checked them out. On impulse, I slipped the chip into my shirt pocket rather than put it back into the camera. I might just want to hold onto that chip. I thought I'd add it to my collection in one of the safe deposit boxes.

I checked the pictures. They turned out perfect. There they sat together, six peas in a pod. They were six of the same person. I was really on to something here, and I knew it. The question was, "What am I going to do with it?" The data that I had compiled so far would read like one of those sensational books about UFOs. I had to do better, if I was going to use this information. I had to fill in some blanks. First, though, I was going fishing.

Everything at home seemed fine as I entered the house. I remembered to deactivate the alarm. It was new, and I wasn't accustomed to it yet. It would take time. I dumped my junk in the living room and headed for the pool. I felt the need for some exercise. After swimming for more than half an hour, I showered and sat down to go through the mail. There was nothing that really needed my attention. I then checked messages on my home phone. There were a few messages, but nothing that required immediate response. I then made a salad and sat down to eat while watching a bit of Fox News. It was all about the economy and politics. Occasionally it would be nice to hear some good news. It seemed like the commentators were always going after each other. The liberals hated the conservatives and vice versa. They both professed tolerance but practiced little of it. I watched awhile and then got bored, so I turned it off and got my computer out. I studied the photos that I had taken at the orphanage. When I blew it up to full screen, I saw something that I had not noticed before. Standing in one of the windows of the orphanage behind were the six boys had been sitting was none other than one Julio Gonzalez, the man who had tried to steal my bag at the airport and then broke into my house. It hadn't taken him long to convince Houston PD that he should be released. He wasn't looking out at me when I took the photos, but was facing into the room, but at an angle. I could see his profile, but was positive that it was him. Immediately I got the chip with the pictures on it and put it in my safe. I would take it to the safe deposit box tomorrow.

The next morning I was at the bank just after opening time. I took care of placing the chip safely in the box and then locked it away. I still had not figured out what I was going to do with the pictures. Without something concrete to support them, they would just look like I was trying to sensationalize the whole cloning thing. What could I find, though? That was the mystery that plagued my mind as I drove home.

Since it was still quite early in the day, I decided to review some more of Doc's notes. I popped the disc into my computer and picked up with the next entry. There was quite a bit of time that lapsed since his last entry. This one was dated June 9, 2009.

Somebody has been looking through my library. Since I keep this research in my hidden floor safe, I am reasonably sure that nobody has found it. I am going to build another secure place for the data so that if they find and destroy this, it will still be available. Jack, you are the only one that will be able to find it. Remember what I always told you about the cross. It is important.

I am more convinced than ever that there is some basis for further study. It seems that I have run into some resistance. I am hiring someone to do some leg work for me. He will have no idea what he is looking for. I'll just tell him to look for anything unusual, especially cases of identical twins, triplets, etc. I'm going to send him to orphanages that are located reasonably close to genetic research facilities to see if there is some evidence of human cloning. What better place to conceal their work.

Wow! Doc had been thinking just like I was thinking. I wonder where his findings would be kept. Probably in that other secure location. I was going to have to figure out where it was and how to get into it. Doc's riddles were making my head hurt.

He was always several steps ahead of everybody else when it came to the thinking department. I never knew anybody to outthink him. He was unparalleled intellectually in my experience.

I continued reading.

I am not going to name the person that I am engaging to do this work. He will be paid in cash so that there is no connection between him and me. That is safer for both of us. He will be asked to supply photos and visible documentation of his work so that all of the information will be verifiable. I don't know how far these people will go to keep their plans under wraps.

It was clear to me that Doc believed that he was onto something that those who were involved would prefer to keep secret. It looked like he feared for his associates as well as himself. His final entry for that date was, "It may be some time before I have anything further to report as this is a fairly extensive undertaking."

It appears that Doc had done more extensive work than I had. It made me wonder what kind of documentation he had hidden in his cache. I really wanted to see it, but first I had to find it. Knowing Doc, that was not going to be a simple task. He loved riddles and was good at solving them. It looked like he had left one for me to solve. One of the worst things about it was that I could not ask anyone for help. I was going to have to figure this out on my own. Well, not exactly on my own. I breathed a prayer for help and wisdom and then went to bed.

I was up with the first light as usual. Today was packing day for my fishing trip. I really could not wait. I had not been fishing for months. The intentions were there, but somehow it was not a priority, and so it got pushed into the background. One thing about making plans with somebody else is that it helps us to follow through. We can disappoint ourselves, but not our friends.

On impulse, I decided to drive to Michigan. It was a two-day drive. My truck was in the garage, so I started to load it with my fishing gear, clothes, and other junk that I wanted to take with me. I was all done packing by about twelve thirty, so I made myself a sandwich and decided to get an early start to Michigan. I set the alarm and then drove out of the garage. I checked to make sure the garage door closed behind me. On impulse, I headed out as though I was going to the shopping area rather than the expressway. I stopped at the post office and set an order to forward my mail to Stone House and then headed north. It was about one forty-five in the afternoon, and I had plenty of daylight. I could probably make it close to Little Rock, Arkansas, before stopping for the night. It felt good to be on the road.

I noticed a white van turned onto the access ramp right behind me, which didn't really mean anything to me at the time. I drove for a couple of hours and then pulled off to stretch my legs, get rid of some coffee, and buy some more. I noticed that that same white van had gotten off at the same exit. Nobody seemed to get out of it. The windows were tinted so I could not see in, but those things registered without setting off any alarm bells. I kept driving into the afternoon. At about six, I was approaching Texarkana. I was making good time. I wouldn't admit to breaking the speed limit, but I was certainly bending it out of shape. On the outskirts of Texarkana, I stopped to gas up and once again to stretch my legs. Again I noticed the white van. Now I was getting a bit suspicious. That was more than coincidental. I decided that my next stop would be one that would flush them out if their intentions were less than honorable. I paid for my gas and intended to pay for another cup of coffee, but the girl being the counter told me to forget it, so I thanked her and headed on down the road.

I drove for about an hour and was well into Arkansas when I saw the sign for a rest area. I didn't really need one, but I needed to draw out my shadow, if possible. I pulled into the rest area very slowly and watched the rearview. Sure enough, the white van was right with me. I walked inside and went into one of the booths. Feeling just a bit ornery, I pulled my feet up so that couldn't be seen from the outside. I heard somebody come moving slowly along the line of booths and pause. Then I heard some whispering. It did not sound like English, but was hard to distinguish. Then I heard footsteps moving slowly down the line of stalls. I sat there in absolute silence. I then heard some agitated conversation that was not English or Spanish. I spoke both of those languages fluently. It sounded like it could be Italian. Some of the words were similar to Spanish. I heard them leave and waited a few more minutes and left myself.

As I walked out into the common area of the rest area, there were only two men standing there. They stood between me and the door. I started walking toward the door, and they blocked my way. They were both larger men than me. I stopped and looked at them. I smiled and asked, "Are you the guys in the white van that has been tailing me since Houston?"

One of the two was older, and he spoke, "We need to talk."

My response was, "If you have a badge, show it to me. If you don't, get out of my way." One of them put his hand on my shoulder. That was a mistake. In less time that it takes to tell it, they were both lying flat on their backs staring up at me. I said, "I'm leaving now and if I see you following me again, I will call the highway patrol. Find yourselves another pigeon." With that, I walked to my car and headed out. I wanted to disable their van, but there were probably cameras in the parking lot. It didn't make sense to get busted for vandalism. I drove a couple more hours and was just west of Little Rock when I pulled off to spend the night.

CHAPTER 9

I was tired and ready to hit the sack. After a quick shower, I turned in and was just about asleep when it occurred to me that the guy back at the rest area had touched me. That would not be significant except that there were tracking devices that could be attached to a shirt sleeve and would not be detectable under normal circumstances. I got myself out of bed and put my clothes back on and grabbed the shirt that I had been wearing earlier outside. I walked across the street to a convenience store. As I walked past the gas pumps, there was a pickup truck with a Montana license plate on it. There was a bunch of junk in the bed. I quietly slipped that shirt into the bed of the pickup. I hoped they were going home. I would have to remember to check my vehicle for a GPS or some kind of tracking device as well. Tomorrow would be soon enough for that. I walked back to my room and slept like a baby.

In the morning, I awakened early. The birds were singing outside my window. Once the coffee pot was going, I took a shower. I sat down with a cup of coffee and thought over what had happened in the past few days. It seemed like a year since Doc's funeral, but it had been just over a week. So much had happened that it didn't seem possible that so little time had passed. I packed my stuff, which didn't take but a minute. After checking out of the motel, I looked for a place to have breakfast. Little Rock boasts a great buffet by the name of Brown's Country Store. I love buffets but rarely indulge myself because of my food allergy. I swell up when I eat too much, and I definitely eat too much at Brown's. Having allowed those thoughts to caution me, I drove to Brown's for breakfast. There was more method than madness to my plan. The parking lot was always full at Brown's. I had a plan hatching in my head. My plan, however, had its priorities. I needed to eat before anything else.

I shouldn't have gone in there hungry. Although I didn't stuff myself, I had consumed enough calories to last me all day and then some. It was the first time that I had eaten at a buffet in months, but it would be wrong to pass up Brown's. I walked out to my truck and started combing it for a GPS. I found it tucked up under the rear bumper. They had put it in with some kind of sticky substance. I looked around the parking lot and saw a big pickup that was hauling a trailer load of pigs. That made me grin. I walked around like I was stretching my legs before starting out again. As I passed the hog trailer, I stuck the GPS up under the fender well. I dearly wanted to see the two stooges when they "found" me. A photo of their faces would be priceless, but the audio would probably be something that you wouldn't want your kids to hear. That made me grin too.

I finished looking my truck over in case they had not been satisfied with just one device. I found nothing more, so I hit the road. I did not expect to see my two friends again for some time. They would find me; they knew too many of the places that I had to show up, so ultimately they would find me, but they were out of the picture for a few days.

The rest of the drive to Michigan was uneventful. Several times I had to chuckle thinking of my "friends" chasing a pig truck. That was just funny, and there was some poetic justice in there somewhere. They were going to know they lost me if they had put a tracker on my shirt because my shirt and the GPS that I took off my truck would be going in different directions. By the time they sorted it out, I would be long gone. They shouldn't bother me until I got back to Houston or when I got back to Stone House. I pulled in to my lake property in Michigan at around ten in the evening. I was road-weary and glad to come to ground. I pulled my truck into the garage, grabbed my overnight bag, and locked the truck. The house was a little musty but aired out quickly once I opened the windows. There was a nice, cool breeze coming across the lake.

There wasn't much in the house to eat. There was bread in the freezer and some canned meat. I made a sandwich and had a glass of water. The water here was excellent. Then I called Mike. I knew he never went to bed early. He would not be able to fish tomorrow because of other commitments. I knew that I had arrived a day early. I told him that I'd just fish here in the morning and get in some provisions in the afternoon. We made plans to meet on the day after tomorrow to float the river and fish for some small mouth bass, walleye, and whatever was hungry.

By the time I'd had a sandwich and relaxed a bit, it was past eleven in the evening and I was very tired. I went to bed thinking that I'd be on the lake in the morning. That helped me drift off to sleep. In the middle of the night I heard something outside and thought that my friends from Texas and Arkansas had caught up with me already. It was interesting how paranoid one can get and how quickly it can happen. It turned out the noise was raccoons in the neighbors' trash. I should have remembered. I turned on the yard light, and they scampered away, but not very far. They looked at me like, "Who do you think you are turning on lights in the middle of the night?" They looked slightly indignant. I no more than turned the light off and they were right back at it. I guess they have to eat too.

The crack of dawn found me awake and putting my fishing gear into my canoe. This was going to be a great morning. The air was cool, but the sun was hinting at coming up and the sky was clear. I slipped quietly across the lake to one of my favorite spots on the lake. I put a tube bait on and tossed it up near some lily pads. It had not been in the water for ten seconds when something hit it. I fought a nice bass to the side of the canoe and measured him. He was just barely legal, so I put him on a stringer. I caught a couple more small ones and then started catching nice-sized blue gills. I caught about fifteen of them that were about seven to nine inches. There weren't huge, but they were nice. I had enough for breakfast and more besides, so I paddled back across the lake and jumped up onto the dock. I secured the canoe and stowed my gear in the shed. Then I quickly cleaned my fish. That took about a half hour. I prepared a couple of the blue gills and half of the bass and broiled them. The others I froze in a bag of water for later use. I wanted an egg, but had not been to the store yet, so that was out. I was very hungry. I ate the bluegill and some toast and thoroughly enjoyed it. Fish never taste better than when they are freshly caught and cooked immediately. The bass I saved for later. Maybe I'd put it in a salad for lunch.

I cleaned up the kitchen and looked at the clock. It was only nine in the morning. I locked up and jumped in my truck to drive to town. I needed some basic stuff to eat. I didn't even have coffee, which was unheard of for me. I guess I didn't plan very well on the way in. I drove to town and picked up some fruit, coffee, some beans, and other veggies. I then headed for the cabin to stow my goodies and plan the rest of my day. Mike called to see if I had caught anything this morning. I told him that I had caught one bass and a few blue gills. He asked if I had eaten them for breakfast, and I told him that most of them were on ice, but I had eaten a couple of the blue gills. We chatted a bit about tomorrow and then he congratulated me on my position at Stone Church. I thanked him, and we hung up.

It was in my mind to do some reading, but the next thing I knew I was waking from an unscheduled nap. Since there was no pressure, it was not a problem. I really don't mind unscheduled naps unless they cause me to be late for something that I need to do. Today, that was not the case. I felt so refreshed. I decided to take the canoe out and try for some late afternoon bass. I had met the morning crew, so it was time to introduce myself to the afternoon shift.

I paddled quietly across the lake and started casting up into the lily pads. That did not produce anything but a couple of very small bass. I decided to try casting out over the drop off and retrieving back toward shore. On the third cast, I tied into a nice bass. It was not a trophy, but it went about five pounds, which was really nice for that lake. I put him on my stringer and kept fishing. Suddenly I had a really hard hit. It did not feel like a bass. It was running deep and pulling hard. My thought was that I had hooked a northern pike. Sure enough, when I got him to the boat, it was pike that would go about thirty-four to thirty-six inches. That was a nice fish. I have caught bigger, but it has been a long time. I thanked him for the fun and let him go. I didn't want to bother to clean a pike tonight. I picked up a couple more nice bass and then got into a school of crappie. I caught my limit quite quickly. It was still about an hour and a half before dark, but I decided to call it a day.

When I arrived at the dock, I cleaned the fish and stowed by fishing gear. I walked back to the dock to be sure that I had secured the canoe and then buttoned things down for the night. I kept about three of the crappie out for supper and put the rest in water and froze them and the bass. I would take some of them home with me. I would have to pack them in dry ice, provided I could find some.

As I was about to start cooking supper, I noticed a vehicle parked down the street from the cottage. It didn't seem possible that those guys had found me already. I walked down to their car. As I approached it, the engine started, so I stood right in front of it so they couldn't drive away. I motioned for them to get out. Sure enough, it was my "buddies" from road. I have to say that those guys were really good. It took them less than twenty-four hours for them to find me. Somebody had access to some pretty sophisticated surveillance or information data. They just stood there looking at me. Finally I asked, "Hungry? I was about to cook some fresh fish. Why don't you guys come inside and have supper with me and you can explain why you are so interested in me?" They looked at each other and shrugged and started for the cottage.

When we got back inside, I opened the package of crappie that I was going to freeze and pulled ten more fillets out. These were big guys and looked hungry. I prepared them in a pan with lemon, salt and a few light spices heated the oven. I then sliced and started frying some potatoes. Just so you know, I fried them with pam rather than oil. I did put a drizzle of olive oil in them. They don't taste right without it. I put some green beans on to heat and then stuck the fish in the oven. In about fifteen minutes everything was ready to eat. I put it on the table, and we sat down. I told them that I always give thanks to God for my food, and they bowed their heads. I admit, I peeked as I prayed. When I said amen, they crossed themselves and said amen too. So I knew where they were from. We introduced ourselves, and I found that they were brothers named Rory and Liam Riley. I asked them what a couple of nice Irish boys were doing following me around the country. They chuckled a bit and then tied into the food. I was right; they were hungry. When they tasted the fish, their eyes popped open. They both said at the same time, "Man, you can really cook!" Then we all looked at each other and laughed. After that, supper was relaxed as we ate and chatted. When we finished eating, they jumped up and cleared the table then washed the dishes. I did some cleaning in the kitchen. Suddenly we were all standing in the kitchen staring at each other realizing that the pleasantries were over and that it was time to get down to business. They acted like they really didn't want to do it.

I said, "Let's go into the living room and sit down. We can talk in there." We walked into the living room and sat down.

Rory cleared his throat and said, "It was really nice of you to invite us in to eat. We were starved and had not thought to bring anything to eat."

"I thought as much," I replied. "I figured if we are going to occupy the same general real estate, we should get acquainted."

Liam said, "You've had some hand-to-hand combat training." It wasn't a question, it was an observation.

I told him, "I was Special Forces." I was quite sure that I would not have to explain that to them, and I was right.

As we talked, they told me about growing up in Boston and being orphaned at the age of ten. After that, they grew up in a Catholic orphanage. They had been adopted by a Jesuit priest who had allowed them to keep their Irish name although he was Spanish. They had grown up in Boston and educated in Jesuit schools. They were both very bright students and had studied at Boston College and then studied at the University in Salamanca, Spain. They both had PhDs and taught at the Boston College and were colleagues of Dr. Lucas's son. Once they started talking, they were very informative. It suddenly occurred to me that the priest that I had seen with Steve Lucas at the church below Stone House was their adopted father. I asked them, "Where does your father live now?"

Rory replied, "He is the bishop over the diocese in which your new home is located."

I responded, "I would very much like to meet him sometime."

"He would like you," responded Liam.

"Look, you guys, I would like to visit more, but I am going fishing early in the morning with an old friend. I'll be getting up at daylight. Why don't you come back tomorrow evening and we'll continue this. I'll even let you cook spaghetti for me, if you want." They both grinned and acted very excited about the idea. "You guys go to town and get what you'll need. I'll be home by about 3:00 p.m. You can take as long as you want to cook then we'll eat and visit some more. Let me suggest that you check into a motel. I'm not going anywhere for a few days." They both laughed and said that they would see me tomorrow and headed out.

CHAPTER 10

I was up at the very crack of dawn and had a quick breakfast. I then headed out to meet Mike. We were planning on getting on the river by six. The section of the river that we were going to fish took about five hours to float and fish. If the fish were really biting, it would take a bit longer. We expected to be off the river by noon or one o'clock at the latest.

It was a really beautiful morning. The sky was clear with no wind to speak of. There was a light breeze that didn't even get down to the river. We could see it rustling the tops of the trees. I caught a nice rock bass on the very first cast. It looked like it would be a good morning to fish. Mike had been my good friend for many years. I had known him for over forty years. We had a lot in common and shared a twisted sense of humor. He was a bit nuts, but I got him and enjoyed his company.

It was our habit to float down the river and fish until we found a good spot and then drop the anchor and fish that spot until the fish stopped biting there and then move on. As we floated, I caught a snag and broke my line. While I was tying on a new lure, Mike hooked a nice small mouth bass. It was about sixteen inches and was a keeper. We got the fish into the boat and then maneuvered it so that we could fish the hole and dropped the anchor. After a couple of casts, I hooked into a nice one too. We got it to the boat and measured it. It was seventeen and a half inches. That was a really nice small mouth. After that, the hole dried up and we moved on down the river. We picked up three more keepers and caught eighty-three fish altogether. Mike had an uncanny ability to keep count of the fish. I never could keep track, but when I was with him, I didn't need to. He always knew how many he caught and how many I caught. He was just a little bit competitive. That is the understatement of the century.

We reached the spot where we left the river at just after one o'clock. I helped Mike load the boat. Since he didn't want to clean the fish, I took them back to the lake house and cleaned them. Rory and Liam showed up right on time. They were in excellent spirits. They went right into the kitchen and started working on their sauce. They had more spices than my kitchen had ever seen. They acted like they knew what they were doing. Once the sauce was cooking, they came into the living room and sat down. They said that it needed to cook for at least three hours, so we had awhile to visit.

I asked them why they were following me. They looked at each other and then started. Liam said, "We were sent to follow you and find out where you went and what you did."

"What would be the point of that?" I asked.

Liam replied, "At first, we had no idea. We were just told to do it."

"Are you the guys that shot at me back at Stone House?" I asked. They looked completely shocked as though they did not even know about it.

Rory said, "We weren't even in the state of West Virginia at that time. We were in Boston. We didn't leave Boston until our father called and said that he had a job for us. That's when we started following you."

I asked them, "Do you know Julio Gonzalez?"

Liam replied, "Yes, we know him. He works for the Vatican as some kind of investigator."

"Yes, I know that. He visited me in Houston and I saw his Vatican credentials." They really looked shocked at that.

Rory said, "He was not supposed to show them to you."

"Well," I replied, "he didn't really show them to me."

"How did you see them then?" asked Liam.

"He tried to break into my house in Houston," I replied. "He underestimated this old man too."

They both grinned and then started laughing. The more they laughed the harder they laughed until they were rolling back and forth with tears running down their cheeks. Rory gasped. "I would have paid a lot of money to see that. Julio is an honest to God tough guy. You must have shocked the you-know-what out of him!"

I replied, "He did seem more than slightly shocked when he came to and was tied to a chair in my kitchen." At that they laughed so hard that I considered calling 911. It really occurred to me that they were in danger of dying of laughter.

"You knocked him out and tied him up?" they screamed between fits of laughter.

"Yes, I did. And while he was tied to my chair, I took his keys and walked down the street until I found his car. I brought all of his stuff in to my house and went through his bags in front of him. In the process, I found his Vatican ID. Once I realized that his Vatican credentials would get him out of any problem with the police, I removed them from his satchel so that the police would hold him. I just wanted a day start on him."

Liam said, "He was really mad about that. He wants to kill you with his bare hands, but I think he is going to be very careful before he tries it again."

They started laughing again. Rory looked at me with a very serious look and said, "You must be really good. He thought that you were asleep and would be disoriented. That obviously was not true."

I told them, "I was trained to come out of sleep ready to fight. That's not something that you ever get over."

"Lucky for you," they said. They asked me what had awakened me. I told them that I had heard a very slight sound. They were really impressed.

Liam said, "Julio said that he did not make a sound opening your door. He said that you are the best that he has ever encountered. He wants a rematch."

"He should be careful what he wishes for," I replied.

"That's what I told him," said Rory, and started laughing all over again.

I really wanted to know why they were following me, so I followed up with them. "Has anybody told you why they wanted me followed?"

"Well, it has something to do with your new position. Our father and others think that your Dr. Lucas had discovered something that he was not supposed to know. They think that you now are in possession of that information. They are trying to keep track of you thinking that you will lead them to the information and they can destroy it."

"I don't have any information that can't be found on the Internet. If he had some kind of empirical proof, I have not found it yet," I replied. I continued, "Do you have any idea who would want to kill me? Somebody took a shot at me. I saw the shooter move from his spot in the bell tower of the church down the hill from Stone House."

Rory quickly replied, "I don't know anything about it."

Liam was silent, and I just looked at him. Finally he said, "I heard Father and somebody talking about it. They thought if you were gone, they would have freedom to search Stone House."

"Was he talking with Steve Lucas?" I asked.

"Yes," he responded.

"Wow," I said, "Doc's son trying to have me killed! That is really bizarre. Did he think that he would have access to the property if I was gone?"

"That was the idea," replied Liam.

"You can let them all know that I have left explicit instructions that Steve was not to be allowed on the property," I told them.

Rory replied, "We already found that out. He tried to go over there as soon as you took off. He almost got arrested. They have armed guards there now."

"Those were my instructions," I told them. "You might let them know that those armed guards are ex–Special Forces guys and are not to be messed with. They will hurt anybody who tries to sneak onto the property. Also, if they take any more shots on or near the property, those guys will find them and they will wish they had been picked up by the cops. Trust me, they will tell my boys everything that they want to know. Do you think that sauce is anywhere near ready to eat?" They chuckled, and we went to the kitchen to cook the pasta and make some garlic bread. Dinner was a smashing success.

When we pushed back from the table, I said, "You guys can really cook! That was some of the best spaghetti I ever tasted."

"Thanks," Rory replied, "but you should taste Father's spaghetti. He taught us, but we could never get it quite right."

"It was delicious!" I told them. They looked very pleased. "By the way, is your car a rental?" I asked them.

"Yes, it is," Liam replied.

"Well," I said, "since you're going to follow me all over the globe, why don't you turn your car in and just ride with me? When I finish my fishing up here, I'm going to drive back to Houston and then back to Stone House. It would save you a car rental and all that driving. We could take turns driving and enjoy some company as well. What do you say?"

They looked at each other, and Rory replied, "We'll let you know, but the idea makes sense."

"I'll be leaving on Friday morning; let me know," I told them. After a short after-dinner visit, they left me to my own thoughts. It seemed a bit crazy to offer them a ride, but it has been said that one should keep friends close and enemies closer. It seems the best place to keep an eye on them was right under my own nose. I hoped that this was good idea.

Mike and I had planned to fish later in the morning tomorrow, so I did not have to go to bed really early. I decided read some more of Doc's journal. I put the disc in the computer and picked up where I left off. This entry was dated August 15, 2009.

I am in receipt of several reports from my investigator. He has secured photos from Catholic orphanages that are close to genetic research facilities. The results of the research is quite stunning. There are identical children in all of the orphanages. They are not, however, twins. There are no less that eighteen identical children in four different facilities. Had we time to inspect all of the potential locations, there is no telling how many of them we would find. I would like to talk with Jack and tell him that his suspicions seem quite likely factual. It doesn't seem safe to share this information right now.

There is no doubt that somebody is doing some serious work in the field of cloning. I am not certain that we will be able to tie this to anybody in particular. It is my suspicion that it has something to do with the Vatican. There are very few entities on earth who have the wherewithal to accomplish this task and keep it so well-hidden. It may be difficult to establish an evidentiary link. Our best strategy may be to try to get a rise out of the Vatican by making them think we know more than we do. I am placing these reports in my new storage facility.

That was the end of the entry. I really needed to figure out how to find that hidden storage area. I put the disc back in its hiding place and went to bed.

The next day was a great day on the water. We caught a ton of fish and got to the point where we were culling the bass to keep only the big ones. We had one that was for sure over five pounds and a couple of others that were close. We could keep five each, and we already had our limit by eleven thirty. We were floating the river and could not get out until we got to the landing where we had left the car, so we were basically captives of the river until around one thirty. I had planned to stay until at least Friday, but as we talked I got the impression that Mike had some things that he needed to do, so I mentioned that I was thinking about leaving early, since I had to move from Houston to West Virginia and had a lot to get done. That didn't even begin to include getting into my new position. I kept my discussions general, as I didn't want to mention any of the "strange" stuff that was going on. He agreed quite quickly to my suggestion, so I'm quite sure that he was hoping to have some free time at the end of the week too. We agreed to make this our last trip down the river for this time and went back to fishing. We had no more than tossed our lines into the river that I hooked a really powerful fish. With small mouth it's hard to tell if it's a big one by the fight. Small mouths sometimes just don't know that they aren't big, so they fight hard anyway. This one, though, felt heavy along with being very strong. When I finally brought it next to the boat, we saw that it was really big. Joe netted it, and it measured twenty-two and a half inches. That was the biggest small mouth I had ever caught on the river. We took pictures and celebrated our moment. Just as we rounded the last bend in the river before the landing, Mike hooked a big one. He brought in another one that was just a bit smaller than my last one. It was twenty-one and three-fourths inches. We both left the river happy that day. We had two nice stringers and had both caught our limit of small mouth bass.

When we landed, it was about one thirty and we were both hungry. We packed up the boat and put our fish in buckets of water and headed into town for a bite to eat before we parted company. As we ate lunch, we recapped that last few days of fishing. We talked and laughed about the trip. Suddenly Mike got very serious. "Is something bothering you?" he asked me.

"There are some things about this new position that have me concerned. I don't know how to deal with a couple of things," I replied.

"Is it something that you would like to talk about?" he followed.

"Not right now," I said. "Sometimes it's better to study a situation until you understand it before talking about it. Do you know what I mean?"

"Yeah, I get it," he replied.

"Just pray for me," I requested. "There is a lot of new stuff coming at me, and I don't know how to handle some of it."

"You got it!" he said. Lunch was over, so we shook hands, embraced, and went back to our lives.

As I drove back to the cabin, I called the "brothers" to let them know that I would be leaving in the morning, if they decided to ride along with me. They did not pick up, so I just left a message.

Since I did not want to carry my disc of Doc Lucas's journals in the car with my "friends" from Boston, I took it up to the post office and sent them to Stone Church via U.S. mail. I sent them overnight and placed a note in there to Jennifer to let her know to lock them up until I got back. I hoped that she would not read the disc. It wasn't that I didn't want her to know what was in them. It just appeared to me that people who were privy to the information contained on the journals lived dangerous lives. I was hoping that I could get more information out of the brothers on the way back to Texas.

I packed my stuff for the trip and hit the sack. I figured to leave quite early in the morning. When I walked out to load my stuff in the car, Rory and Liam were waiting on the porch. I had not heard them arrive. I shook their hands and told them that we'd get coffee on the road. We loaded our stuff and hit the road. It was still quite early. We were driving out of the driveway at five forty-five in the morning.

Our first stop was a gas station and convenience store. I filled the gas tank and bought the biggest coffee they had. It was my good fortune that they had dark roast, which is my favorite. In ten minutes, we were on the road. Even though I was travelling with men who were not to be trusted, it was nice to have some company. I thought maybe I could weasel some information out of them if I asked the right questions.

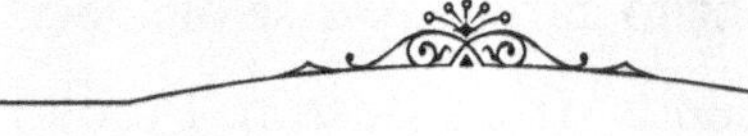

CHAPTER 11

We drove until lunch time and had reached the middle of Illinois. We stopped for lunch and to gas up. I was getting sleepy, so I asked if one of them would like to drive. I told them to just follow the directions given by the GPS and it would take us home. Rory volunteered to drive, so I sat in the back seat and dozed off. I was awakened by a ringing phone. Liam answered and put it on speaker so that Rory could hear it too. The voice on the phone had a strong Italian accent. They talked for a few minutes and then switched to Italian. Maybe they were thinking that I would not understand. It never pays to underestimate your opponent. I was fluent in Spanish, but got along just fine in Italian as well. They were talking about something that the brothers were supposed to be doing. It dawned on me that they were talking about me. The voice on the phone said in Italian, "He knows too much; he has figured it out." Liam and Rory insisted that "he," meaning me, had not figured anything out. That's why I say that it pays to keep your mouth shut and your ears open. I'm not sure that I had it figured out, but was quite sure that I was making progress. I continued to pretend to sleep as I listened to the conversation. The voice on the phone started talking about another "he." What I heard was, "He is almost ready to start." Although I didn't know who was starting and what he was starting, I was getting curious. Then the voice said, "He'll be thirty in seven more years. That is when it will begin." They sounded very excited about it. I had an idea what was going on, but no proof of anything.

The thing that bothered me was the question, "How can the Catholic Church be cooperative in bringing the antichrist into the world?" That didn't really stack up with some of the leaders that I knew in the church. There were good men in the church who would have no part in such a scheme. There had to be an explanation. I just had to search for it. It was very hard because everything had to be done under such a cloak of secrecy that it was difficult to make an overt investigation. They ended the conversation without saying anything else that sounded significant.

I gave them about fifteen minutes of thinking that I was asleep and stirred myself. "It would be nice to make a pit stop, if you guys don't mind," I said. Rory started looking for a gas station so we could take a break. I noted that he had been driving for about two hours. I had slept a good part of that time. After our break, I decided to try to engage the brothers in conversation. "So who put you guys on my trail, anyway?" I asked.

"Our boss," they replied.

"Who is he?" I asked them.

"We can't say; he doesn't want to be in the middle of this," was the response.

"He doesn't want to be in the middle of what?" I asked.

"What is going on," they replied.

"Well, what might that be? I have no idea what is going on," I responded again.

"Well, this whole thing," was their reply.

"You'll have to pardon me, but I have no idea what you are talking about," I told them.

"You're in the middle of it. How can you not know?" Rory said.

"I'm in the middle of what?" I asked again.

"We're not supposed to talk about it," Liam said.

"If you guys won't talk with me, how am I going to find out what I'm in the middle of?" I was getting confused.

They looked at me with searching looks, and finally Liam said, "We can't give you any details, but the gist of it is about the second coming of Christ. There is a group of people who are trying to facilitate that. Most, but not all, of them are from the Catholic Church, and the Vatican really wants to keep the project under wraps until the time is right."

I was both stunned and enlightened by this revelation. It made sense based on what Doc Lucas and I had surmised and uncovered. I tried to draw them out with more questions, but they had said all that they were going to say. That explained the motives of at least some of the church leaders. They thought that they were going to help God bring about the second coming of Christ by cloning his body from the DNA on the shroud of Turin. It was a scripturally ignorant, crazy, and naïve plan, but it was also quite brilliant from one point of view. It would cause a great resurgence in the Catholic Church and really all of Christendom. It made a lot of sense from the church's point of view. In my opinion, it made no sense from a scriptural point of view. There was nothing in the Bible that pointed to a second coming of Christ as a baby. The angel told the apostles in Acts that he would return in like manner as they had seen him go up into heaven. No doubt there were people in this movement that knew that. We humans are masters of rationalization, though. We can believe something to be true, especially if it is more convenient for us that it be true rather than false. Wow!

Rory said, "You are very quiet all of a sudden."

"Well, you have given me a huge idea to wrestle with. I need time to process it," I replied.

He smiled. "We have plenty of time, so wrestle away. While you're wrestling, we need to get some gas." He pulled off at the next exit to get gas. To the credit of Rory and Liam, they insisted on paying for the next tank of gas. At least they weren't freeloaders. I was beginning to like these guys. I had to remind myself that they really weren't friends. I must stay on my guard. It would be dangerous to become careless. I hated to have to live like that, but my training told me to be very careful. My feelings so much wanted to trust these guys, but my gut told me not to do that.

While Rory was pumping gas, I went inside and used the bathroom and grabbed a cup of coffee. I took over driving when we left the gas station. We were now in Arkansas and cruising along. I thought that it was unfortunate that we were going to miss Brown's Country Store at mealtime. I really didn't need to eat at a buffet, but that did not in any way diminish my desire to do so. Breakfast was my favorite meal there, though. There was just no better place on the planet to eat breakfast. They simply had everything an American man could want for breakfast on that buffet. You could not leave that place without eating too much. We drove through the Little Rock area without stopping at the buffet—a lost opportunity.

As I drove, I noticed that Liam and Rory were glancing at each other and were apparently trying to communicate without saying anything. Liam was riding shotgun, and Rory was directly behind me. Liam was sitting in the front seat with his body partially turned to the left. He still had to turn his head in order to look at Rory. I could see him gesturing in my peripheral vision. I decided to be proactive. "Do you guys need to have a private conversation? Liam, you're going to have a kink in your neck tonight if you keep twisting around. I can stop and give you a few minutes, if you'd like."

Liam's look at me was not nice. "No, we're fine," he said. He did turn back around, though. I decided to be even more watchful. That look that Liam had given me gave me cause for contemplation. Something was up. As we drove, Liam was texting. Finally about five thirty in the afternoon, he asked me if he could plug his phone into the power outlet as the battery was low. I told him he could and showed him where to plug it in. He plugged it in, and I pulled off the highway in Texarkana to have some dinner. I wasn't very hungry, but I wanted to be out of the vehicle for a little while.

There was a tension in the air that I had not felt since the brothers confronted me at the rest area on the way from Texas to Michigan. We went into the restaurant, and I purposely left my phone in the car. As we sat down, I commented that I had left my phone in the car. After ordering, I excused myself and went back out to the car to retrieve my phone. While there, I quickly dumped the text messages on Liam's phone, which was still charging. The second to the last one was from somebody named "The Sword." It said, "Kill him." Now I was both stunned and clearly apprised of the situation that I was in. Now, at least, I understood the tension in the air. They were probably as conflicted as I would be in the same situation. They were beginning to like me and bond with me. I was going to need to be hypervigilant.

I walked back into the restaurant and actually felt cheerful. I thought that I would have to put on an act, but it wasn't necessary. I felt happy, upbeat, and cheerful. They, on the other hand, did not. It was a miserable meal for them. I felt a bit sorry for them. I told them that we might as well stay there for the evening. There was a Best Western Motel there, and I usually like to stay in their motels. We got our rooms and headed for our separate places. I noticed that Rory had taken special notice of which room I was in. Once I got in my room, I called the office and told them there was a strange smell and I would like to change rooms. They told me that they only had a room on the top floor a long way from my friends. I told them that was fine, and I changed rooms. I made a couple of phone calls and then called the desk and asked them if they had surveillance on the hallways and parking lot. They said that they did. I went to bed and to sleep. I was tired, and nothing was going to keep me from sleeping.

About three in the morning, there was the sound of an explosion. I ran to the window of my room and looked out. I saw Liam and Rory running toward my SUV. They were trying to open it with an electronic key, but it would not open. When they hit the unlock button, I noticed that the tail lights of another vehicle a few spaces down from mine were lighting up. They noticed it too and looked very confused. I went down to the parking lot. When I got down there, they were putting their bags in the vehicle that they had keys for. When they looked up and saw me standing there, they looked like they had seen a ghost. I said, "Are you boys leaving so soon?" They came at me together. Rory took a swing at my head, and I ducked under it and hit him in the solar plexus and then gave him and uppercut to the chin for good measure. He went quietly to sleep. I then turned to Liam who was setting up to come at me with a club. I slapped it aside and jabbed him in the throat. He immediately dropped the club and grabbed his throat. He was choking, but was breathing. The sound of his breathing was awful. I put a sleeper hold on him and laid him down beside his brother. On a sudden impulse, I took both of their phones. I might be able to find some phone numbers or other data on them. I then went back up to my room. It would be better if the police had no idea of my involvement in the fiasco. As I entered my room, the black and whites were pulling into the parking lot. I was pretty sure that they would find the keys to the car that the boys were about to steal in Rory's pocket. I was also pretty sure that they would find guns, explosives, and burglary tools in the possession of the brothers. Those boys were going to be occupied for some time, I was thinking.

In the morning when I went down to the dining room for breakfast, I heard the story. It seemed that they broke into the room that I had vacated and killed the man that was staying there. They then attempted to steal his car, but somehow they were rendered unconscious and the police found them lying on the ground with all of the incriminating evidence including the keys to the victim's car, which they were apparently planning on stealing. The theory that the police were working on was that they had started fighting over who was going to drive and knocked each other unconscious. It was a bit outrageous, but they could not come up with a better explanation. The police were charging them with first degree murder, attempted auto theft, and breaking and entering. There would probably be other charges as well. My thought was that they were not long for this world. It was doubtful that their failure would be allowed by their handler whose moniker was "The Sword."

Before leaving, I carefully checked my vehicle and clothes for more tracking devices. I found three and surmised that there may be more than that. Without an electronic bug finder, it was not likely that I would find all of them. I did the same thing with them as I had done before. I tossed them into the back of a pickup that was parked close to my SUV. Maybe I'd get lucky this time and they would follow the devices instead of me.

The police were questioning the people who were out and about during the incident. Since nobody had seen me out, I did not volunteer any information. My neck felt like it was far enough out anyway. I didn't feel like adding to its exposure. I was very sorry for the man that was killed and very happy that it wasn't me.

I was minutes from Texas and could not wait to get back there. I headed for Houston with grim thoughts in my head. Those guys really meant business. After the good times we had together, they had really tried to kill me. I could not get that thought out of my head as I drove. They made a real effort to kill me on the orders of this guy called "The Sword." I needed to figure out who he was and why he thought it was important to rub me out. That was the second serious effort to kill me. It suddenly occurred to me that they might think that I was dead. Rory and Liam might not tell them that they had failed. The news said that an unidentified man had been brutally murdered in a Texarkana Best Western. Maybe if I laid low, they would think me dead and I could work with some freedom at least until they figured out that I am not dead. I left my SUV in the parking lot and took a taxi to the bus station. I called a towing service from the bus depot and asked them to pick up my SUV. I arranged to pick it up after a few days. I then bought a ticket to Houston from Texarkana and settled onto the bus trying to get comfortable. I was soon fast asleep, and the bus wound its way across the Texas countryside.

Arriving in Houston, I took a taxi home. When I arrived there, I told the taxi driver to drop me in the alley behind the house. Once I paid him, I went in the back door. If they were watching my house, I didn't want them to know I was there yet. There was nobody visible at the front, but they could do surveillance with cameras and watch from a distance. I wanted them to think I was dead, if possible. I started packing the stuff that I wanted to take with me. This was going to have to be a light load. I would try to get back down in a few months once this all blew over. I packed three large bags and a backpack. I then called a car rental and leased a car to drive back to Texarkana and get my SUV. It probably was much ado over nothing, but I had stayed alive in the Special Forces by trusting my instincts and leaving nothing to chance. I called another taxi and told them to come through the alley and then carried my stuff out to the back gate. When the taxi came, I told him to take me to the car rental place. He started to turn to pass the front of the house, but I told him not to do that. We went to the car rental and avoided the front of my house.

I put my stuff in the rental vehicle, for which I paid cash and headed for Texarkana. I stopped at the towing yard to pick up my SUV. The guy that had picked it up from the hotel was there. He asked me if I was in some kind of trouble. I told him not that I know of and asked why. He said that there were a couple of guys going over my vehicle and looked like they were about to break into it, but did not get the chance because he picked it up. I thanked him for that and paid him a $50.00 tip with the instructions that he should not answer any questions about me or about the truck. He grinned and said that he would handle it. I called the rental agency and told them that they could pick their car up at the tow yard and gave them the address. I then headed out hoping that I had avoided detection.

CHAPTER 12

Once on the road, I called the office at Stone Church and updated them as to what was going on. I told them that I was alive and on the road, but there had been an attempt on my life and I was going to take a couple of days to get there. Jennifer said something that gave me some food for thought. She said that just before Doc Lucas passed, they had thought that somebody was following him. He had even thought of hiring security, but then he passed and it was no longer an issue. It started me wondering if, even though he was very old, he had died of natural causes or had he been murdered. Maybe I was just paranoid because there had been two attempts on my life in the past few weeks. I had forgotten about the shot that somebody took at me just after Doc's funeral. I really needed to do some serious thinking about the whole situation.

Rather than heading east toward West Virginia, I drove southeast toward the Gulf of Mexico. I remembered a small town in Mississippi with a hotel right on the beach. That would be a good place to spend a few days for some contemplation and trying to sort out what was going on. I called the office again and told Jennifer that I would have my phone turned off for a few days but would be in touch via a landline. I told her that I would give her a number where I could be located in case of emergency.

The road to Mississippi was long, but I arrived there in the late afternoon. The people at the hotel remembered me and were happy to see me. I told them that I was paying cash and did not want to leave a credit card on file. I put my extra cash in their safe and kept $1,000.00 cash for any expenses that I might incur during my stay. I then went to my room to relax. After reading for an hour or so, I walked across the street to a restaurant that had great sea food and had a dinner of blackened red snapper and a nice salad. After eating, I took a moderately long walk on the beach. The beach had always been a good place for me to think. I sat down on the sand and just let my mind drift. It felt good not to feel pressure. Even though I knew that nothing had changed, I felt at peace. Even though feelings aren't particularly reliable, it was nice to relax even for a short time.

Upon returning to my room, I showered and went to bed. Sleep came quickly, and the next thing that I remember, the sun was peeking through the shades and calling me to come out and enjoy the morning. I started the coffee pot and then took another shower. Sitting down in my boxers and a tee shirt with a cup of coffee, I started reading in the book of Isaiah. As I read chapter 54, the verse just stood out to me: *Isaiah 54:17, "No weapon forged against you will prevail, and you will refute every tongue that accuses you. This is the heritage of the servants of the Lord, and this is their vindication from me, declares the Lord."* I stopped reading and just sat back to mull over what the Lord was saying to me. It was encouraging to know that I was not alone in this quest. Sometimes in the rush of life, we forget that God knows where we are and that he is planning for us.

I put on a pair of jeans and some sandals and took another walk on the beach. I did not see anybody. There was nothing but the sounds of the sea. Oh, and the gulls, they let me know that I was not alone. They were a noisy bunch. They came over by where I was and circled around until they realized that there was no free food here and then went elsewhere. I guess even nature will take easy pickings, if they are to be found. The gulls had the good sense to get back to work almost immediately. Too bad people didn't show such good sense sometimes.

At around eleven, I wandered back to my room. I sat down and turned on Fox News to see what was going on the world. There was nothing new really. There was constant friction between liberal and conservative politicians. It seemed never ending. History was full of the same fight, the same rhetoric, and the same dirty tricks. Solomon was right. There really was nothing new under the sun. Since I hadn't eaten any breakfast, I went over for an early lunch at around eleven thirty.

After eating, I felt like I needed some exercise, so I went down to the pool and did a few laps. I probably swam for at least a half hour. While swimming, I realized that I had not called the office to let them know how to get in touch as I said that I would do. I had seen a pay phone down the block, so I decided to make the call from there. I took some cash from my room and bought a prepaid calling card then called the office using the calling card. I told Jennifer where I was and how to get in touch with me. She was to call the desk at the hotel and leave a message for me that Barry Mack had called. The name was random, and I chose it because there was absolutely no connection with anybody I had ever known. If I received such a message, I would call Jennifer as soon as I could.

That call started me thinking about Doc Lucas. Could his death have been something other than what it seemed? He was the most unsuspecting person ever. He loved and trusted people. It made me wonder if he had gotten too close to something that somebody didn't want people to know. I started laughing at myself. I was sounding like a ten-year-old reading a Hardy Boys novel. What I needed to focus on was the promise of Isaiah 54:17 and just trust in the Lord. I knew that in my head, but my feelings were still unsettled by the events of the past few days. It was crazy that in the past couple of weeks there had been two serious attempts on my life. These people, whoever they were, meant business. That was unsettling.

While I was at the coast, I decided that I would take advantage of the fishing. I called a made reservations for the next morning for a fishing excursion in the Gulf of Mexico. That would be fun. I then went for another walk on the beach, ate a light dinner, and went to bed.

I awakened with a start and realized that I had been dreaming. There were three different dreams with the same scenario. In the one that I remembered most clearly, I was watching a white rabbit running from a coyote. The rabbit hid in several places, and each time the coyote chased it out. Finally the rabbit hid under a large rock, and as long as it stayed under the rock it was safe. I got the point. I decided as soon as I finished my fishing excursion on the Gulf of Mexico, I was heading back to Stone Church and Stone House.

I was at the dock very early the next morning. Going out on the gulf was both a rare pleasure and an unexpected one. The weather looked perfect; I was looking forward to a great day of fishing. As it was an all-day trip, I kept my hotel room for one more night. We headed out for the oil rigs where we usually started fishing. By the end of the day, I had caught a couple of nice tuna, a couple of mackerel, and a few smaller fish. I was going to have to buy a cooler and some dry ice to pack them in to take them home. It was way too nice a catch to leave behind. I especially like freshly caught tuna. The canned stuff is okay, but freshly caught is wonderful. I couldn't wait to get some of it on my grill.

Once back on land, I packed the fish in Ziploc bags and a large cooler with dry ice. I wrapped and taped the cooler to add a little more insulation and keep any moisture from leaking out. Then I showered and hit the sack. I'd be heading home in the morning.

CHAPTER 13

I was on the road by around seven in the morning. It felt good to be headed home. What really felt good was the peace that I felt. It seemed like the dreams that I had were assurance from the Lord that there was safety at Stone House and Stone Church. The trip could have been a one-day trip, but there was really no reason to push hard. I decided to drive up through Chattanooga and visit some of the Civil War sites there. They always fascinated me. As I was driving, I noticed a white car behind me that seemed to always be there. Whenever I sped up, they sped up. Whenever I slowed down, they slowed down. Whenever I stopped for at a rest area or for gas, they stopped too. The windows were darkly tinted, so I couldn't see who was driving or if there was one or more people in the car. I decided to play a little trick on them.

I got between two trucks so they couldn't get in without being very obvious. As we approached an exit, I pulled out like I was going to pass the truck in front of me. When we were almost on top of the exit, I cut across in front of the truck and took the exit. I had seen the white car pull up behind me trying to catch up. He did not make the exit. I didn't need gas, but I topped off my tank. I also swept my vehicle again for GPS devices, and once again, I found one. That I dropped in the bed of a random pickup. After about a fifteen-minute stop, I started down the road again. As I passed the next exit, I saw the white car pulling back onto the highway behind me. Now, it was clear that they were following me again. It had not been a coincidence. I didn't care anymore. I was just going home, and they could find me there anyway.

At around five in the afternoon, I pulled off the highway and pulled into a Holiday Inn. I went in as though I was registering. What I did was actually ask for directions. After about ten minutes, I came walking out putting something into my shirt pocket. It looked like I had registered. Then I pulled around the side and parked. I went into the side entrance and walked back up to the lobby. From the end of the hallway, I could see the white car parked under the awning. Looking around the corner, I could see the person who was registering. It was Steve Lucas and a priest whom I had never seen before. I went back to my car and drove away while they were registering. I got onto the highway and went back the way I had come to the first exit. There I registered at the Quality Inn. I told the lady at the desk that somebody had messed with my vehicle at the last place that I had stayed. She told me that they would keep a close watch on it for me. I took my overnight bag up to my room and then jumped into the pool for a half hour of swimming. Then after a quick, light dinner, I was ready to call it a day. On a whim, I took a burner phone that I had bought as an afterthought a couple of days ago and called back to the Holiday Inn where I had pretended to register. I asked for the room of Steve Lucas. After two rings, he answered. I just hung up. They probably had not even figured out yet that I wasn't there. I slept well as awakened refreshed the next morning.

I had set the alarm for four in the morning, so I was on the road by five. If all went according to plan, I'd be home at around noon or shortly thereafter. That was my goal, at least. The rest of the trip was uneventful, and I did not see the little white car again. For the life of me, I could not understand why Steve Lucas would be following me. That made no sense, at all. I decided to do some research on him. I knew him, but knew nothing about him. Maybe there was something significant that I didn't know about him. If there was a hidden secret, I would find it. It was just a matter of turning over enough stones.

Everyone at the church was happy to have me back. I told them that I had not been able to complete all my business in Houston, due to circumstances beyond my control. Since it was not really pressing, I'd take care of it later. I had people caring for my place. For now, that was going to have to do. I spent the afternoon catching up on what was going on and returning phone calls. I asked Jennifer if there has been any unusual inquiries or strange people hanging around. She said that there were a couple of guys that had been in church for the past few weeks. They were very exclusive and seemed to just be observing, but did not participate beyond the minimum of going through the motions of worship. She had never seen them before, and she knew nearly everyone who attended regularly and most of the regular "occasional attendees." These guys did not fit in either category. I asked her if she knew whether or not they were on any of the video footage from the services. She smiled and pulled out a sheet of paper that she had printed from the video. There was the priest that I had seen with Steve Lucas just before somebody took a shot at me and another who I did not recognize. The priest was not dressed like a priest. He was wearing a pair of jeans and a golf shirt. I kept my thoughts to myself and went into my office. Well, they could report that they found me.

I sat down at my desk and decided to start sorting through Doc Lucas's papers to see what needed to be filed and what, if anything, I needed to work on. As I worked, I found a curious reference on a calendar that I found tucked away in the desk. It simply said Mark 13:12 with the word *treachery* written beside it. The date that it was written on was about a year before Doc's passing. Having my curiosity piqued, I picked up a Bible and found the reference. What I found was the words of Jesus talking about conditions in the last days. Specifically it said, *"Now brother will betray brother to death, and a father his child; and children will rise up against parents and cause them to be put to death."* I stared at that verse, read it over several times, and then read the context. The context was Jesus talking about the last days. He was warning his disciples how things are going to change before he returned. What was Doc trying to say? Was this for me or just a random thought that he had jotted down because of something he had noticed? I decided to check out Doc's schedule of appointments for the day on that little calendar. I walked to Jennifer's office and asked her for Doc's schedule for that day. She said she would look it up and e-mail it to me. I walked back to my office, and by the time I sat down, the computer was letting me know that I had a new e-mail.

I popped the e-mail open, and the only appointment on the schedule was a delegation from Boston College including his son,

Steve. The subject of the meeting was not noted on his calendar. I walked back to Jennifer's office and asked if Doc took notes on his meetings and where they might be. She said that he always did and that they were filed. He had used notebooks for those meetings. They were filed by date, and I would need to locate the one that contained the date in question. She offered to do it, but I told her that I'd take care of it myself. She showed me where the stacks were, and I found the notebook that I wanted. After sitting back down at my desk, I began reading the account of that meeting.

My son, Steven, came to my office with three of his companions from work. At least one of them was a priest. The others may have been priests incognito or colleagues of Steven from the university. It was not clear to me who they were. The only two who spoke were Steven and the priest. He told me his name was Father John. When I addressed him as John, he replied, "Most people address me as Father." To which I replied, "I have two persons in my life whom I have addressed as Father. One is my biological father who is deceased. The other is my heavenly Father who is not. You are not either one of them, so I think not, sir. I will address you by your name, if you please." I saw a flash of anger in his eyes, which he covered very quickly.

The conversation continued in general terms until I quite pointedly asked them what it was that they had wanted to discuss with me. They looked at each other, and then Steven spoke for them. He said that we had some common interests in research and they would like to "share" research materials. I asked what the subject of their research was and what made them think that I had any interest in it. Steven spoke again saying that there were certain websites that they monitored to see who visited them because of the contents. They had noticed that I had visited several of these websites. They even knew how much time I had spent on them and what I had downloaded. It appeared to me that they had placed some kind of spyware on my computer in order to keep track of the sites that I visited. I asked pointedly, "Have you been spying on my computer?" Steven's response was, "What makes you think that?" I replied, "Because you know more about my cyber research than I have shared with anybody else."

They quickly changed the subject thinking that they would disarm me with their charm, and they were very charming. John quickly stepped in and began to talk about how well-appointed my office was, etc. I was gracious and thanked them explaining that I had designed the room myself. They asked if they could see the plans, to which I responded that I had destroyed them after the remodel project. They also asked what contractor had done the work. I did not tell them, but it had been done by an Israeli friend of mine who specialized in "special projects." His name was Moshe Bengurien and was a younger cousin of

David Bengurien. Moshe was a believer in Jesus and a dear friend. I trusted him, and that was why he was hired to do the remodel project. This I had told nobody, not even my family. There are things about this office that need to be kept secret from everyone except the pastor of Stone Church.

I sat back in my chair after reading this entry. What was the secret and how would I discover it? In all of the reading that I had done, I had not noted anything that hinted of a secret in the office. I had found the floor safe because Doc's attorney had shown me where it was and how to open it. The safe was so expertly concealed that one could be standing on top of it and not even know it was there. What else could there be? I decided to keep on reading.

The account of the meeting went on.

Steven was getting agitated because he knew that they were not getting anywhere. "Dad," he said, "it would be in everyone's best interest to work together and share information." I replied, "Son, you have not yet divulged the subject of the research that has brought about this visit. Why don't you tell me what it is we're talking about?" He looked disgusted and said, "You know very well what we're talking about." I replied, "You tell me just the same. It works better for me if all the cards are on the table. I want to know what you're holding before I show mine." He replied, "It doesn't work that way, Dad." To which I responded, "If it doesn't work that way, then it doesn't work at all." About that time, John stepped in with this remark, "Dr. Lucas, there are subjects that are of such sensitive nature that we need to know who knows what. If we are not able to reach a working relationship, we would have to consider alternative actions." I looked him right in the eye and told him, "You are wasting your breath threatening me. I survived some of the hottest action of World War II by the grace of God, and you don't scare me, not even a little bit. This interview is over. Kindly remove yourselves from my office and property." I then buzzed Jennifer and told her that our guests would be leaving and would she please escort them out.

I sat for nearly an hour after they left pondering their words. It occurred to me that they were afraid of what they thought I knew. That more than anything fed the idea that I was on the right track. How interesting that a seemingly random remark from Jack during one of our skull sessions would bring such a reaction. This will certainly require more work. I wonder what alternative actions the priest John was considering.

That ended Doc's entry regarding that meeting. Call me crazy, but it made me wonder if Doc had been murdered. I know it sounds crazy, but there had been two attempts on my life since his passing. Somebody did not want me to find out what Doc knew. If they couldn't stop Doc from working, the next best action would be to keep the data in a "lost" state. It made me more anxious to find out what else was in Doc's papers. If, and it's a big if, he were murdered, was Steven involved? Did he even know what happened to his father? Did he suspect? More questions were rattling around in my head with very few concrete answers volunteering for consideration.

It was past dinner time and I was hungry. I went to the kitchen and made myself a salad with some leftover chicken in it. After eating that, I watched TV for a while and then went to bed. My head was tired. Tomorrow I needed to do something for exercise. Maybe I'd get myself a bicycle. In these hills, that would be great exercise. I fell asleep and dreamed of coasting down those long hills.

The telephone awakened me from a deep sleep. I looked at the clock, and it was around three in the morning. I was pretty sure that the call was not from a friend. Nobody that knew me and liked me would call me at that hour unless it was an emergency. Then I noted that the call was from out of the country. I answered with a simple hello.

The voice on the other end was heavily accented and sounded Spanish or Italian. "Is this Jack?" came the question.

"Yes, it is. Who are you and why would you be calling me at 3:00 a.m.?" was my response.

"You know me as 'The Sword.' That's really all you need to know," he said.

"What do you want and why couldn't it wait for a more convenient hour?" I asked.

His response was, "This time is perfectly convenient for me."

"Well," came my slightly sarcastic reply, "as long as it's convenient for you, everything is fine. What do you want?"

His reply was a little strange, "Your friend, Dr. Lucas, was fearless, but not very cunning. You, on the other hand, are both, and that is an interesting combination. The way you disposed of the brothers from Boston was brilliant. I must say that I have completely underestimated you. Trust me, that won't happen again."

My question was, "Why does any of this even matter? I don't know you and have no idea as to why you are interested in me."

He came back, "I think that you do. Your friend passed his church and property over to you for a reason. I don't know what it is, but I intend to find out."

"Why?" I replied. "There is nothing interesting in that. We had been friends for years."

His reply told me that he had been studying on this for some time. "Until just a few years ago, everyone believed that he would pass his church and property on to one of his sons who had followed him in the ministry. Then he suddenly started doing a bunch of research, which caught our attention as we have similar interests. We noted his research as he was repeatedly visiting websites that pertain to areas where we have vested interest. We started monitoring his communications and noted that his communication with you increased after and during that time as well. We are sure that this has something to do with you, and we intend to find out what it is."

I needed to stall and try to derail this guy, if possible. It seemed that it would not be easy to do that. "What research are you talking about?"

"Oh, I think you know," he responded. "Your recent trip to Mexico and your interest in cloning indicate that you are picking up where he left off. You, however, are much more clever than he was. The brothers from Boston thought that they had you completely hoodwinked. They were making fun of how gullible you were even inviting them to ride to Texas with you. They thought that they were watching you," he said with a chuckle. "The thing is, Jack, those boys were very well-trained operatives. They were some of my best, and you handled them like school boys. To say that I am impressed is truly an understatement. Those boys are going to prison for a long time. I can't help them because of the way you set them up. I could not have done any better myself, probably not as well. My compliments."

"Well, thank you, I think," I said. "What now?"

"We need to know what you know for one thing," he replied. "We want to share information as it is only fair to give something to get something."

"I'm willing to work something out, but the truth is I have not found all of Doc Lucas's notes and research on the subject, whatever it is."

He laughed right out loud at my intentionally sophomoric attempt to cover that fact that I had divulged that there was material. "What do you mean?" he asked.

"Whatever Doc Lucas found out was of such a sensitive nature that he didn't put it in files. He hid it somewhere, and I have not yet figured out where it is."

He asked, "Why would he do that?"

It was my turn to chuckle. "You would have to have known Doc. He was a puzzle. He had the most brilliant mind of anyone that I have ever known."

"Coming from you, that is high praise," he acknowledged.

"It's true. I'm not just being modest. You could learn from him just by listening to him breathe. Did you guys kill him, by the way?" I had been trying to derail him, and that just about did it.

"What do you mean?" he demanded.

"It was just a question," I said. "Doc thought that his life was in danger because he refused to be intimidated by your delegation. Your reaction really answers my question. Really the next issue is, why would you do that?" I asked.

He hesitated and then replied, "We thought that one of his sons would be in charge of the property and that we could get in there to find Dr. Lucas's research notes. We never anticipated his move in making you his heir. That caught us completely by surprise."

"Me too," I replied.

He chuckled at that and replied, "The boys told me that you are a truly humble, unassuming man. I believe that this did take you by surprise. However, that doesn't really get us to a solution for our problem, does it?"

My guarded reply was, "I'm not even sure that I understand the problem. That seems like the obvious first step before looking for a solution. Oh! By the way, you didn't answer my question about Doc Lucas. Did you guys kill him?"

He paused for a long few seconds and then replied, "Since I am out of your country and you don't even know my name, I guess I can be candid with you. We presumed that his death would not raise any suspicion. We wanted free access to his study, so, yes, we hastened his already imminent demise. Again, we did not anticipate that you would become involved. This has caused much distress on our end. It was quite smart of you to change all of the locks."

"So who actually poisoned him?" I asked.

"How did you know it was poison?" he replied.

"Don't change the subject again, please. Just answer the question," I demanded.

He said, "I can't tell you that without putting him in jeopardy."

"Yes you can," I replied. "I'm not going to do anything with the information. I don't want to draw attention any more than you do right now. I have other ways of settling accounts."

"What do you intend to do?" he asked.

"Well," I replied, "I'm not going to kill him. I don't do an eye for an eye."

He answered, "You wouldn't believe it if I told you."

I answered, "It was Steven, wasn't it?" I heard a sigh on the other end and knew that once again, I had hit pay dirt. I told him, "I'm not going to say anything to the authorities about it, but don't be surprised if somebody else figures it out. People aren't as stupid as you might think…not all of them anyway." We chatted a while longer, and he asked me about sharing data. I told him that I would think about it and that he could call me back in about a month during working hours. That really made him laugh, then we hung up.

By the time we finished our conversation, it was about five o'clock and we had been talking for a couple of hours. I decided that I was going to figure out who he was before he called again. It was not my job to make them pay for murdering Doc Lucas. God would take care of that. I just wanted Steven Lucas so nervous that every time the phone rang, he would think it was the police. He deserved that and more. I wanted him so scared that he couldn't work, think, or do anything. I owed Doc that much, and I was pretty good at psychological warfare, if I do say so myself.

CHAPTER 14

The next morning when Jennifer came in, I was waiting for her. I was very curious about Doc Lucas's health the last few months. According to her, Doc was actually quite healthy for a man ninety-seven years of age. She said that he was taking one pill for high blood pressure and one pill to keep his cholesterol under control. Apart from that, he took several natural vitamins and one baby aspirin per day. I asked her if there had been an autopsy ordered. She said that there was quite an argument in the family regarding that very idea. Several wanted to do it, but Steven argued against it. He kept saying that at ninety-seven it was probably his heart, and why go through all that. He finally won out, and the others gave up. Then I asked her who was the last person to see Doc alive. She wasn't sure, but that Steve had visited his father the day before his death. The visit was in the late afternoon, and she did not know the subject of the conversation. Then I asked her if Doc had ever expressed to her that he thought somebody might want him dead. She indicated that he had never said anything to her about it. As far as I could tell, the only indication that Doc left that he was in some kind of danger was in his notes that he knew I would see. It was also apparent that he suspected that his son, Steve, was involved. He would have been on his guard, so how did they do it?

On impulse, I called Jennifer to my office. When she came in, I asked her to look around and see if there was anything new or unusual in the office. She looked around slowly and said that everything looked the same. Then she looked on the desk, and suddenly she pointed at a carved wooden horse. She said, "That was not there before. I think that Steven brought it to Doc that last time he visited. You know that Doc loved horses?"

I replied, "I do remember that. So this is new then?"

She nodded, "Yes, I think it is." She started to pick it up.

"Don't touch it! It might not be safe," I told her. She looked at me like I was nuts, so I had to tell her. "Doc may have been murdered for his findings during some research that he was doing."

She looked at me with horror on her face. "How…why? Why would anyone do that?" She gasped.

"It looks like he may have uncovered something really huge while researching something, and he must have made somebody nervous."

She looked at me and then asked, "Are you in danger too?"

Again circumstances made it necessary for me to tell her something. "There have been two attempts on my life since taking over Doc's work," I told her. She was speechless. I told her, "You have to be absolutely silent about this to anyone but me. I will try to tell you what I can, but I do not want to endanger you and your husband."

"Are we safe, now?" she asked with eyes that looked as big as saucers. She looked so much like a scared little girl that it made me smile.

I replied, "I don't think that you are in any danger, because you don't know anything. If strange people are hanging around, I'd like to know about it. Under no circumstances is Steve Lucas to be allowed anywhere near this place. I'm going to have cipher locks placed on my office and living quarters. We will do what we can to protect ourselves, but I am not going to become a recluse!"

Her final word was, "Wow!" after a long stare at me. She returned to her office, but it was doubtful that she would get much more work done today.

I went back to my desk, Doc's desk, and went back to work. After a while, I sat back and surveyed the office. There was something that I was missing about this office. I studied the walls, shelves, floor, and finally came to rest on the fireplace. It was massive and beautiful. The hearth was a half circle and was stone. The rest of the floor in the room was marble and was exquisite. I got up and walked over to it. As I examined the fireplace, I could not see anything unusual about it. It was decorated with carved crosses. The largest and most elaborate was in the middle. It was a beautiful piece of work. I then walked around the office and examined the artwork. There was nothing really valuable, but Doc had a good eye for art, so it was tastefully decorated. He had liked good harmony in music, and his taste in art ran the same. There was much harmony in the artwork in the office. It was a pleasant place to work. That's the way Doc had intended it.

After a while, I sat back down and went back to work. I was scheduled to preach Sunday morning, so I worked for a couple of hours doing sermon preparation. My mind kept returning to Doc's journals. It seemed they were not going to leave my mind until I did some more reading in them. I put my sermon preparation aside and opened the floor safe. After extracting the next of the journals, I closed the safe. I started reading, picking up in the next journal. It read like this:

> It seems quite certain at this point that somebody is trying to clone Jesus from the DNA on the shroud of Turin. It is also apparent that they have had some success. It is unclear how successful they have been because the project is kept very secretive. The generations of identical boys that we have seen and photographed indicate that the project has been going on for at least fifteen to twenty years. It is reasonable to presume that it has been going on longer. It is also possible that there have been some successes in the process. It is possible that they could have a viable clone in his/its late teens or early twenties. Which would mean that he/it could be introduced to the world at any time. If the powers behind this project follow the biblical pattern, he would not begin any overt public life until around his thirtieth birthday. This is all speculation. It may be that they already have a viable clone nearly old enough to introduce. Maybe these others are for spare parts or just to be sure they have one. Given

the church's stance on abortion, they would feel obligated to keep the clones alive.

I sat back and rested my eyes. My mind was not at rest, however. Doc had put a lot of thought into his notes. He both discussed what he knew and what he suspected. It was not very scientific. In this case, however, it was important to be thorough in discussing the possibilities. I also puzzled over where the photos might be that he had noted in his notes. I really wanted to see them. I continued reading.

In reading Ezekiel recently, I came across verses in chapters 34 and 37 that are intriguing in this context. Ezekiel 34:23 and 24, *"I will establish one shepherd over them, and he shall feed them—My servant David. He shall feed them and be their shepherd.²⁴ And I, the Lord, will be their God, and My servant David a prince among them; I, the Lord, have spoken."* In chapter 37 of Ezekiel the restoration of the Davidic kingdom is mentioned again in the specific setting of the restoration of Israel and Judah in the last days. Verses 22–28 discuss this clearly.

I quickly opened my Bible to review these passages. This is what I read:

Then say to them, "Thus says the Lord God: 'Surely I will take the children of Israel from among the nations, wherever they have gone, and will gather them from every side and bring them into their own land; and I will make them one nation in the land, on the mountains of Israel; and one king shall be king over them all; they shall no longer be two nations, nor shall they ever be divided into two kingdoms again. They shall not defile themselves anymore with their idols, nor with their detestable things, nor with any of their transgressions; but I will deliver them from all their dwelling places in which they have sinned, and will cleanse them. Then they shall be My people, and I will be their God.

'David My servant *shall be* king over them, and they shall all have one shepherd; they shall also walk in My judgments and observe My statutes, and do them. Then they shall dwell in the land that I have given to Jacob My servant, where your fathers dwelt; and they shall dwell there, they, their children, and their children's children, forever; and My servant David *shall be* their prince forever. Moreover I will make a covenant of peace with them, and it shall be an everlasting covenant with them; I will establish them and multiply them, and I will set My sanctuary in their midst forevermore. My tabernacle also shall be with them; indeed I will be their God, and they shall be My people. The nations also will know that I, the Lord, sanctify Israel, when My sanctuary is in their midst forevermore.'" (Ezekiel 37:21–28)

After pondering these passages for a few minutes, I returned to reading Doc's journal.

It appears that there are forces at work to try to clone Jesus and reestablish the throne of David. I wonder if it is possible that they are trying to clone King David as well. Could it be the false prophet and the antichrist? Is that even possible? Who would be involved in such an undertaking? Is there technology available that would even do this? I have more questions than answers at this point. That they are cloning is a fact. Who they are cloning is the question.

I put the journal down then. This was too much to absorb at this point. It seemed like every time I picked up one of Doc's journals, the water got deeper. It occurred to me that, although they ostensibly had different agendas, both the Catholic Church and the Zionists have interest in seeing the Messiah reestablish the Davidic throne in Jerusalem. How strange would it be if they were working together? They could never let that come to light as they were pretty much avowed enemies per conventional wisdom. What if they had found common ground? The Catholic Church may be thinking that they are helping to facilitate the second coming of Christ, and the Zionists could be thinking that they are bringing back the "kingdom." As bizarre as it sounded, the more I thought about it, the more possible that it seemed. They would certainly make strange bedfellows. I quickly discarded that metaphor. They would make a truly unholy alliance. What if stronger forces were subverting their efforts for another more sinister purpose?

When it comes to cloning, we really don't have very much information regarding the soul of the clone. Since the clone is not born of a union between a man and a woman, there is some question about the personhood of the clone. Since the cloned person is an exact copy of the tissue donor, would a clone even have a soul as we understand the soul? It is clear that originally God breathed life into Adam and he became a living soul. The established plan for procreation is also clear in the Bible. We know that each human is a unique, living soul. What we don't know is what happens when a being is brought into existence via an unnatural means such as cloning. It seems impossible that the cloned person can have an exact copy of the soul of the original tissue donor. It begs the question, which borders on a theological conundrum? Would the clone be an easy mark for demon possession? Would he have a will of his own or be like a zombie of some kind? Is the present-day fascination with the undead a precursor to a race of cloned individuals? There are just too many unanswered questions regarding cloning. It was hard to know what to expect. One of the difficulties that I was facing is that I did not even know where to start in resolving some of these questions.

I clearly needed a breather. My brain felt like it was being crushed. I looked at the clock and noted that it was about eleven thirty. I hopped into my car and drove to a Denny's that I had seen out near the expressway. After ordering a cup of coffee, I sat back to relax a few minutes. I overheard a couple of older gentlemen talking about small mouth bass fishing. That, naturally, snagged my attention. They were talking about fishing in the Monongahela River. I tuned into their conversation as fishing was my most enjoyed diversion from the pressures of working. They were talking about floating the river starting up river from Fairmont and floating down through the city. They had recently scored a nice mess of fish doing that. As I was always concerned about eating fish taken from rivers in industrialized areas, I decided that it would be wise to check out whether or not they could or should be eaten. They were leaving and I had finished my coffee, so I headed back to Stone House.

As I drove into the driveway, I thought that I saw a figure move into the shadows, but was not able to distinguish what or who it was. I drove into the garage and closed the door. When I stepped into the house, I did not turn on the lights. I moved to a window overlooking the driveway and watched. Soon a man stepped out of the shadows, looked around, and walked down the driveway and off the property. I wondered what he was doing there and then decided to check the security tapes to see if I recognized the person. Upon viewing the footage, I noted that the figure looked like a female. Based on the contours of the body lines, it clearly looked like a female. I had an amusing thought. I wondered in passing if they were now training and deploying "ninja nuns." With that amusing thought in mind, I hit the sack. It was about one in the morning.

CHAPTER 15

I was at my desk by seven the next morning. The coffee was hot and strong, and I felt refreshed and ready to tackle the day. With a good night's sleep and the perspective of a new morning, the problems of last night looked about the same to me. There were still questions to which I had no answers. Today I was going to start working on the ones that I could. The woman that I saw sneaking around the property still had me stumped. I had looked at the footage on the security system. The face was indistinct. I decided not to worry too much about it, but to keep my eyes open. I had checked the doors and windows. There was no evidence that anyone had sneaked in. Besides, the security system was not activated, so I was quite sure that there had been no breach. I had no idea who she was or what she wanted, but since I could not resolve the issue right now, I put it aside to work on something else.

After three hours of scouring the Internet for articles on whether or not a human clone would have a soul as we understand it and reading several, I came to the conclusion that there was no consensus on the subject. Some were convinced, without any evidentiary support that they certainly would have a soul, and others just as convinced with about the same lack of evidence that they would not have. It seemed that both the philosophers and the theologians were floundering with consistent leaping of intellectual and moral gaps without evidentiary bridges. The call could go either way, but it was primarily a matter of opinion. I decided to spend the afternoon searching the Scriptures to see what might be found there.

After a salad and a cup of strong, hot, black tea, I went back and sat down at my desk. I decided to start with a review of the meaning of the word *beast* in the Apocalypse. The word *beast* that is used to refer to the antichrist is *therion*. It is a word that refers primarily to a wild animal. There are some human references in Greek literature always meaning a brutal, savage, bestial, and ferocious person. Again, based on the actual evidence, the call could still go either way. The fact that the antichrist is referred to as "he" indicates that he will be presented in human form. One could theorize, however, that as Christ was God in the flesh, the antichrist could represent Satan in the flesh. There is some indication that this is to be the impression given if not factually true. It appears that the antichrist will be Satan's effort to copy the "God Man" by creating a "devil man." This would be a false representation as Satan does not possess God's power to incarnate himself. Satan has always lusted for God's throne. It looks like he is trying to steal the inheritance of Christ by making his own bid for supremacy via a false, demonic "messiah." What more convincing way could there be than to clone the physical body of Jesus and inhabit that body with himself? It would appear to be the "son of Satan." Such a ruse could indeed deceive many, possibly even the very elect.

I sat back in my chair. The thoughts that were flowing through my mind were giving me a chill. It was depressing to think that such a thing could be going on and nobody the wiser. It did appear, however, that something like this was, in fact, happening. I would not say that all of the thoughts that had come to my mind were accurate, but I was quite sure that there was some basis in fact for them. There was something going on. I recalled what the two brothers had told me when they thought that they were going to kill me. The idea of some of the participants was that they were going to facilitate the second coming of Christ. Why they thought that God needed their help, I could not comprehend. It appears to me that they were being duped by higher and more malevolent influences. The participation of the church lent some legitimacy to the whole operation. In addition, the church had centuries of operating in secret and keeping things hidden from the world. There was nobody more adept at that.

As I sat there pondering the idea of a Satanic "messiah," it occurred to me that there was also a counterfeit Satanic trinity in the dragon, the beast, and the false prophet. Even if they could not clone the body of Jesus, they could produce a clone and say he was Jesus. How would anybody know the difference? If they made more than one clone, it would be easy to fake the "head wound" that made it appear that the beast recovered himself/itself from death. Even though it would all be smoke and mirrors, many would believe because people believe what they see. They may sell the idea of the miraculous by saying the reincarnated body of Jesus had the same power as the original. Many would believe that. It's funny how little evidence people need when they want to believe something.

I looked at my watch, and it was around six thirty. I decided to go grab a bite of dinner at one of the local restaurants. I was thinking that Italian food sounded good, so I checked online for local Italian restaurants and selected one. When I arrived there and was seated, it became obvious that it was a good selection. The place was quite full with people coming and going and wait staff scurrying around with their trays and plastic smiles. I placed my order and sat sipping my diet Coke with lemon and just generally watching people with nothing special on my mind. I noticed a lady come in. What had caught my eye was the way that she walked. She walked with a distinctive gait that I had seen before. She gave me a sharp look, so I smiled at her and then she was led to a table and seated. She was a fairly young lady; one would guess her age at late twenties or early thirties. She appeared to be quite fit. My veal was delivered, and I settled in to enjoy dinner. Giving the lady no more thought, I finished dinner and left for home. This was Saturday night, and we had services tomorrow. I was tired, so I headed for home. I stepped into the church and checked to make sure all was as it needed to be and then went into the house. After making sure all was in order including locking the doors and setting the alarm, I went to bed.

I was weary, so I did not read before going to sleep. As my mind relaxed I felt myself slipping into that almost-asleep-almost-awake place when my subconscious mind flashed the front of my house before me. I saw the same scene I had seen when I saw somebody sneaking around. In the dream, the person had a distinctive gait, just exactly like the lady that I had seen in the restaurant earlier in the evening. Sleep fled from me, and I lay there pondering what, if anything, this might mean. I decided that early next week, I was going to sweep the front of the house and, in fact, the entire property for cameras and listening devices. As strange as it seemed to me, somebody appeared to be watching and listening to what was going on around here.

The next thing I knew, it was morning and the sun was streaming in my window. I looked at the clock and it was 6:47 a.m., so there was plenty of time. I had lain awake a long time last night thinking. Normally, I could empty my mind and drop off to sleep quickly. Sometimes it was more difficult. Last night was one of those. I don't even remember getting sleepy and dozing off. My mind had run the gamut before shutting down for sleep. The question that kept arising in my mind was, what had I gotten myself into here? There was no really clear, complete answer to that.

I put on my robe and grabbed a cup of coffee from the kitchen. I had set the coffee to kick on at six thirty, so the pot had just finished brewing. I walked into my office and walked to the window, which offered a nice view of the valley below. The river was visible below as well as the town. I could see the bell tower of the Catholic Church from my window. To my left, the mountain rose up and the corner of my office was built into the side of the mountain. As my eyes swept the valley, they picked up a movement in the tower of the church below. I stepped back from the window and grabbed my binoculars and walked to the other end of the house to a window facing the same direction. Standing back from the window, I carefully scanned the tower and the area around the church.

As I watched, I saw someone move forward becoming visible behind the balustrade. The person was watching my office window with binoculars. I had to chuckle at the irony. They were watching where I was not, and I was watching them from a point that they were not watching. This was craziness. I could close the shades, but that would alert them that I had noticed that they were watching. It wouldn't matter much, but if they didn't know that I knew they were watching, I could continue to watch them. That could be entertaining at the very least. If I could find some unobtrusive spot in the house to do so, it would be nice to have a high-powered lens pointed at the bell tower so I could see who was watching without spending all my time looking through binoculars.

I showered, dressed, and had a bite of breakfast. Although it was a bit early, I decided to go over to the church. I enjoyed watching people coming in on Sunday morning. The church was about half full when I saw a now familiar figure walking into the entry hall of the church. I noted that unusual gait and knew before I could see her clearly that it was the lady from the restaurant last night. Without giving the idea much thought, I approached her with my right had extended. I smiled and said, "Good morning! My name is Pastor Jack. I'm the executive pastor here and am very pleased to welcome you here this morning. What is your name?"

I saw a familiar look flash into her eyes like that of a trapped animal. She quickly covered and smiled brightly although not very sincerely. "Good morning to you, sir! I am Sarah Harris and I am pleased to meet you."

I replied, "Enjoy the worship time this morning. If you ever need anything, I am at your service." She thanked me and went into the sanctuary and sat down. I had noted an accent that sounded like a Spanish accent, but could not be certain. It was slight, but notable. I had not noticed a wedding ring, so the name Harris raised a question. I wondered what she had been looking for that night when I saw here slipping away from the house.

The morning worship service went by in a blur. I was in a zone, but it was a zone far away from Sunday morning in America. I was so lost in thought that the closing of the service startled me. After greeting the folks that attended the morning service, I wandered back over to the house and threw a pork chop on the griddle and made a quick, very simple salad. There were some leftover veggies in the refrigerator that I stuck in the microwave with a small dollop of fake butter. By the time the pork chop was ready, everything else was too and I enjoyed a quick and satisfying lunch. Following lunch, I went for a walk along the streets. It felt like I had not done anything but work for weeks. That was not true, but that's the way it made me feel. Somewhere along the walk, I decided to have a talk with Doc Lucas's son that taught at Boston College. It seemed like somebody needed to get some things straight with him. I called him and asked him if I could come and see him. We set an appointment for Tuesday for lunch. I decided to drive rather than fly. I wanted to have some time to think.

The next morning I loaded my stuff in Doc's Caddy and headed down the road for Boston. It was not an unpleasant drive. I went north to Pittsburg and then turned east and headed across Pennsylvania. This was certainly beautiful country. I arrived in

Boston late afternoon and secured a motel room for myself. After a light dinner of tilapia with rice pilaf and salad, I retired early to be rested for tomorrow.

Steven and I met at the appointed time. I was right on time and noted that he was already seated at the table. He stood as I approached the table, and we shook hands. He did not seem to display the animosity that I had seen earlier. He had been angry and under lots of stress at the funeral. We chatted in a civil manner as we ate our lunch. Finally he asked why I wanted to meet with him. I told him straight up that I was fairly sure that his father had been poisoned and was surprised to learn that he had argued strongly against an autopsy. "What are you saying?" he asked.

I responded, "I'm not saying anything, but I am here to ask you if you suspected that your father had been murdered and if so, why did you oppose the autopsy?"

He dropped his head and then looked up at me sadly. He said, "My father had the most incisive mind of anyone that I have ever known. When we were children, we could never fool him. He could always see right through our charades. He was the same way when he started researching something in the Bible. He mentioned to me about the conversation that the two of you had several years ago regarding the cloning of the physical body of Jesus and its potential use by the antichrist. I was intrigued myself at first. When Dad started studying the subject, it became clear that there were forces that did not want him or anyone digging around. I learned that some very powerful people in the Catholic Church were a part of this group. They started asking me questions about what my father was doing. I, of course, had no idea, but they asked me to try to find out. You know that Dad was very tight-lipped when he was studying on something. I tried to talk with him, but he only spoke to me in generalities. When I reported this back, the 'powers that be' were not pleased. They asked me if we could hack his computers. I told them that I was not comfortable with that, but they pressed. I told them that I would not participate, but would visit Dad and take one of them with me to meet him. They were going to try to put some kind of spyware on his computer. We did make that visit, and Dad really liked the guy that went with me. The three of us had some great talks. Soon after, they came back and said that there was nothing on the computer that indicated that he had any information. They were sure that there was another computer. I told them that I had never seen one. I checked with my brothers and sisters. None of them had ever seen another computer either. This was just a few months before Dad passed."

I asked him, "Did you make another visit to your dad's place with any of your colleagues?"

"Yes," he replied. "About a week before Dad passed, we went again."

"Did anybody take him any food or anything?" I asked.

"Yes, one of my colleagues took him a package of cookies from Israel. Dad really liked those cookies."

"Had the package been opened when you went back for the funeral?"

"They were gone," he replied.

"Do you think that they poisoned him?" was my next questioned.

"I do think so," he replied, "but I can't prove it."

"How would your family feel about exhuming the body to find out?" I asked.

"I don't know," he replied. "What good would it do?"

"Well, it would not do your father any good, but it would prove to us that he was venturing into territory that was scaring somebody," I said. "Additionally, it would open a murder investigation, which would not be all bad. That might serve to scare them even more."

"Why do you want to scare them?" he asked.

My reply was, "Only because that is their stock in trade. I like the idea that we can serve them some of their own soup, so to speak."

He chuckled at that. "You've got guts, I'll give you that. No wonder Dad liked you so well. You remind me of him."

"Whether you meant it or not, I consider that very high praise. Thank you," I replied.

He looked at me for a long moment and then said, "Dad told me that you have the rare combination of high intelligence, unconventional thinking, and a humble spirit. Dad was rarely wrong about people. Thanks for being his friend as he grew old."

It was my turn to stare. "You have got to be kidding me! Those were some of the greatest times of my life when we would sit and talk. Your dad never failed to surprise me with his vast knowledge of any subject that we would broach. I was honored that he would want to take the time to talk with me."

Steven had a tear as we said goodbye. "I'll check with my family and see what they say about exhuming his body. I'll let you know," he said.

"Thanks. I hope to see you again soon," I said and walked away.

Two days later I received the news that Steven had been in a very serious automobile accident. He wasn't dead, but was badly injured and would be months recovering. The idea that somebody had overheard our conversation or he had let something slip to the wrong person occurred to me and then persisted in the back of my mind. There were too many strange occurrences for this to be coincidence. Whatever was going on, I had the feeling that I had not yet touched the mother lode. I wished that I could find Doc's hidden trove of research data, but so far, I had not been able to find it. I decided that I would not push any more for an autopsy. It would endanger too many other people. I pretty much had my answer. We just couldn't bring anyone to justice. That matter would have to be left to God and his time.

CHAPTER 16

I awakened with pregnant nuns, hit squads, the suspected murder of Doc, and the subsequent injury of Steven Lucas rolling around in my head. It was quite likely that Steven was not meant to survive. None of us, however, can account for the plans and purposes of God when we make our plans. It was apparent to me that there was a reason that Steven's life needed to be preserved. God had a purpose for him to continue on the earth. No doubt he was pleased to still be in the land of the living.

After some debating back and forth in my head, I decided that I would not visit him at this time. If my contact with him had endangered his life, then it would not be a good idea to make matters worse by showing up now. I decided instead that I would go fishing. I had been wanting to try my hand at the river, so I made arrangements to be free for at least part of the day, loaded my canoe and fishing gear, and headed down to the river. I put in and immediately started upstream. After paddling for about an hour, I picked what looked like a good spot and started casting both into the current and toward the shore. Several small bass let me know that my choice of bait was acceptable, but no big ones had yet offered. One of the great things about fishing is that it requires a certain amount of concentration. There weren't a lot of random thoughts running through my mind as I fished. I always found this quite therapeutic. It was hard to read the river, control the canoe and fish while worrying or thinking about other things.

It took about two and a half hours of slowly fishing down the river to get to where I had started. Along the way I had dropped anchor several times in likely spots and had been rewarded by a couple of nice bass. They weren't huge, but they were respectable. Another boat came by, and the fisherman asked how I was doing. I lifted my stringer for him to see. He seemed quite impressed and said that he had only caught small ones in these waters. The two that I had caught were about sixteen inches. That didn't seem big to me, but I didn't know the waters. I thanked him, and we passed on to continue our fishing. I looked up at the bank and realized that I was directly below Stone House. I could see my study window from here. My eyes casually scanned the shoreline, and I noticed what looked like an inlet or channel that looked like it lead inland from the river. It wasn't very big, but I noticed it. It crossed my mind that it would be something to check out sometime. About that time, I hooked a fish that felt big. I set the hook and quickly dropped the anchor. This one did not want to go home with me. He was voicing his protest in a most physical way. I finally brought him alongside the canoe and netted him. He was a bigger fish. I measured him at twenty-one inches. That made me smile, and I decided on that to head in. I had drifted about a half mile past the landing, so I turned upstream and paddled back to the landing.

As I unloaded my canoe and stowed my gear and the canoe in the truck, there were several people looking over my catch. One gentleman told me that it had been a long time since he had seen a catch like that come out of that part of the river. He also told me that a bunch of guys from the area had coffee every Tuesday morning and invited me to join them the following day. He gave me the location, and I told him that I would try to make it. We shook hands, and I started to get into my truck. As I did, I looked up to the street above where a bridge crossed the river and there was Sarah Harris watching me. I smiled and waved at her. When she saw that I had spotted her, she casually turned and walked on across the river. I seemed like she was trying to avoid me, which I found rather odd, but people will be people.

I headed home and cleaned my fish. I had four nice small mouth bass. I put them in Ziploc bags with water in them and put them in the freezer except for one fish, which I sprinkled with lime, and seasoned it with some salt and pepper. I added a couple of my favorite seasonings to it and put some olive oil in a pan and heated it. I chopped a little bit of onion and green pepper and tossed them in the oil and let them brown a bit and then put the two fillets in the pan. I did not want to overcook the fish. It was better, in my opinion, to just sear it well on both sides. The flavor was better. I put a couple of pieces of Ukrainian bread in the toaster and took the fish out of the pan along with the onions and green peppers. I took some cottage cheese out of the refrigerator and served myself a couple of tablespoonful of that, buttered my toast, and then sat down to enjoy fresh fish for lunch. It was really delicious, if I do say so myself. I have come to realize that everybody thinks their cooking is the best because they make food in their own favorite ways. I have no illusions that I could open a gourmet restaurant, but I surely did enjoy my lunch.

As I returned to my office, it occurred to me to try to figure out who it was that was behind this whole thing. The guy who called me and had said that he would call me again intrigued me. Who was this guy and why was he so certain that I knew something that I clearly did not know? I sat down at my computer and logged onto a website that listed cardinals of the Catholic Church. I did not see anyone who made me suspect that he was the one I was seeking. Then the thought occurred to me that someone working on such a clandestine project would probably not be listed on the websites. I started looking back through the listings of up and coming priests from the past. I was pretty sure that I was looking for a Jesuit, so I stayed in that vein. I went back ten years but didn't find anybody that popped for me. When I went back fifteen years, I saw articles by and about a young priest by the name of Alfonso Xavier Ramos from Spain. I read his articles, and he was truly brilliant. In reading his articles, I could almost hear his voice. I googled him and found that he was elevated to cardinal about twelve years ago and then just seemed to disappear. There were no more articles about him or by him in the Catholic publications. I thought that I had found my guy. It turned out that along with being a priest and a cardinal, he was also a medical doctor trained in biogenetics. His scholarship was clear in his writing, but his intellectual pedigree was impressive as well. I knew that he was going to call me back soon. I was going to have a surprise for him.

I looked at the clock and noted that I had worked right through dinner. It was ten thirty, and I was both hungry and weary. After a quick salad, I retired for the evening. I dreamed of a red bull with big brass horns that looked like they had been honed to needle sharpness. He was bellowing, snorting, pawing the ground, and shaking his head. His eyes were positively evil and hateful. I lay awake for a while after the dream thinking that he was not an enemy that I wanted to have. It might be wiser to keep what I knew to myself. The next thought that I had was an intense desire for a cup of coffee.

It was Tuesday morning, so I decided that I'd go have breakfast with my new friend that I had met when coming off the river. I wanted to meet that group of fishermen and find out where the better fishing spots were on the river. None of them would give up their best spots. Of that I was certain.

I drove to the restaurant, and as I walked in, I spotted my new friend at a table in the back with a group of around six or seven. As I walked back there, my friend spotted me and jumped up. "Hi!" he said, "we were just talking about you."

I responded, "I knew that I needed to show up to defend myself." That brought a chuckle around the table.

We introduced ourselves. The man that I had met at the river was Bill. The others were Frank, Charlie, Will, Sam, Hank, and Shorty, who was around six feet four inches. I figured there was a story behind that name. He saw me looking at him quizzically and grinned. "I'm Shorty, because I was the smallest boy in my family."

I told him, "You read my mind."

He laughed and responded that he gets that a lot. He said, "I'm just used to being called Shorty. My name is actually Harry, but Shorty will do. Bill tells us you caught a nice mess of bass just around the landing."

"I guess I did all right, but I don't really know the river yet," I replied.

He laughed again and said, "At that rate, by the time you learn the river, you'll be skunking all of us."

My response was, "That is very doubtful, but I'd take it." That brought another chuckle around the table. We seemed comfortable with each other, and we started chatting and drinking coffee. The waitress came over, and we all ordered breakfast. One of the guys asked me what bait I had used to catch those bass. Since I had brought a few of my favorite lures along (homemade, by the way), I passed them around for the guys to see.

They looked them over and then asked me how I fished them. One of them started to pass it back to me, and I told him, "Keep it. I want all of you to have one. They have worked well for me, and I think they will work well for you too."

Frank spoke up and said, "Most fishermen don't share their secrets."

I responded, "Do you really think that river is going to run out of fish because seven more people have my favorite bait?"

They laughed and all thanked me. We then started talking about fishing spots. They all shared with me some of the better spots. I would need to get a bigger boat to access some of them, but thought that it might be worthwhile to do so. While we were eating, I remembered the spot below Stone House that looked like an inlet. I asked about it. Bill replied, "It is an inlet. It goes to a boathouse that is cut into the stone base. Doc Lucas kept his boat in there."

I was a bit taken aback and said, "Did you know Doc Lucas?"

They all responded in chorus, "Of course, he was part of our group. "

Then Frank asked, "How did you know him?"

I replied, "We have been friends for years. He was my theology teacher, and then in years later, we became friends. We used to get together every year."

Charlie said, "You're that Jack! You're the new pastor at Stone Church!"

I raised my right hand and replied, "Guilty as charged."

Hank, who had not said much, looked at me and said, "It's like you belong here!"

I smiled at him and said, "I hope you all feel that way because I have really enjoyed this time. Knowing that you were friends of Doc just makes it better. I need to go now, but I'll see you here as often as I can make it. Thanks for the invitation."

As I drove back to the house, I was lost in thought. There was a lot going on that I just could not figure out. That had been a really good time. A vagrant thought wandered through my mind. I wondered if there was a spy in the fishing group. I doubted it, but I would have to be careful what I said. That was probably a prudent policy to practice everywhere with everyone. I did not know who I could trust, so it was best to keep my own counsel until I did know. Doc must have lived a very lonely existence when it came to his research. It occurred to me that only once a year was he unguarded. It would serve me well to emulate his example. It was tough though. A load was easier carried when there was a partner. Then the Lord reminded me that he was my partner on the road and the he always carried more than his share of the load. That helped me; it really did.

CHAPTER 17

The phone was ringing. I thought it was a dream. I awakened a bit disoriented, which was very unusual for me. Finally I realized that it was actually my phone. I looked at the clock as I picked up the phone. It was three twenty-seven in the morning. I had gone to be at around midnight, so I had not been sleeping very long. I said, "Hello, this is Jack."

The voice on the other end was familiar with a strong Spanish accent. "Hello, Jack. Are you well?"

I replied, "As well as can be expected at three thirty in the morning!"

"I am very sorry," he apologized. "Should I call back at another time?"

I responded, "No, Alfonso, I'm awake now. Or do you go by Xavier?"

There was a stunned silence on the other end for longer than I expected given the polish that I had observed in this man previously. "You must be confused," he said a little too emphatically.

I responded, "I guess that put you off your game just a little, right?"

He paused again and sighed. "You are really good," he said with some admiration in his voice. "How did you figure it out?"

I explained, "Well, I was pretty sure that I was not going to find your name on some Vatican register. I did look, however. The real search started as I went back through graduating classes of the Catholic universities looking for someone who had some distinguished academic achievements and had entered the priesthood. The list was rather short. Then I looked for priests who had been elevated to cardinal and then just dropped off the grid. I found a shorter list. A couple of them were deceased. I found all of the others working somewhere in the church. Only you remained alive and unaccounted for as far as a stated work for the church. Since I had eliminated all of the others, you were the last man standing."

He exclaimed, "That must have taken you forever!"

"Well, not quite, but it did take a long time. I am a pretty good researcher, though."

"Obviously!" was his response.

The cardinal said to me, "I hear that you are quite the fisherman."

That pretty much confirmed to me that Sarah Harris was a plant. "I guess Sarah reports everything, right?"

He said, "She is very zealous. We teach our operatives that any little thing could be important. She says that you are a superior fisherman. You were catching nice-sized bass in a part of the river where most fishermen don't bother to fish anymore."

I said, "Do you know what beginner's luck is?"

"Yes", he replied, "I am familiar with the expression, but I don't think it applies in this case. It appears that you know exactly what you are doing in all of the pursuits of your life."

"Do you enjoy fishing?" I asked.

He replied, "I really do very much enjoy it. Why do you ask?"

"It had crossed my mind that, since I know who you are anyway, we should meet. We could go fishing and discuss whatever other business we might have," I said.

He replied with what sounded like true regret in his voice, "If I were to do that, I would have to admit to my subordinates and my superiors that you have unmasked me. That would not be good for either one of us. I am sorry that I must decline to accept your invitation."

I replied, "I get it. You know what you're doing and whom you have to satisfy. I still have not located the mother lode of Doc's research. By the way, I would suggest that you layoff Stephen Lucas. He was shocked when I told him that his father had most likely been murdered. He did not even suspect. He would have never initiated anything, had I not spoken with him. If he doesn't pursue it, I won't either. Part of me tells me that the family has a right to know, but another part tells me that we would needlessly endanger more of them. What do you say?"

He replied, "I can't protect him, but I won't go after him either."

"Fair enough," I replied.

His next question was regarding Doc Lucas's research. "Where have you looked for the research?"

I replied, "Not to be unkind, but that is none of your business."

He chuckled a little and replied, "At some point, it will have to become my business or it will be out of my hands. There are people looking over my shoulder. They are very powerful people. Let me emphasize powerful. They are patient, but they won't wait forever."

"Well," I replied, "they are not going to come in and start tearing my home and my church apart looking for something that may not even exist."

"Oh, it exists," he replied.

"How can you be so sure?" I asked.

He replied, "Your friend told a couple of his sons that he had found some astounding data, but was not sure how to put it to use."

I said, "I have not found it yet. I have looked every place that Doc stored notebooks and have found nothing in the category of data that you have suggested he had. I have keys to every door on the property and have looked inside every door. There is not a key that I have not used to see what was behind it. There is nothing. Maybe the information died with Doc."

He chuckled again. "You don't believe that yourself. Doc was way too careful for that. He put it somewhere. If there is no key, then the key is in your head or in his notes. Something that he said to you or wrote will be the key to finding it. We could hypnotize you to extract it."

"Not in this lifetime!" was my instant response.

He laughed right out loud. "I'm not even sure that you would be susceptible to hypnotism. You're much too hardheaded. Jack, would you allow our people to look through the notes that you have already reviewed?" he asked me.

I responded, "No, but I might consider letting you personally look at those notebooks."

He quickly replied, "I can't do that for the aforementioned reasons."

"You could come incognito," I suggested.

"I don't know how that would work." he said.

I decided it was time to wrap up the conversation. "You think about it and let me know. You obviously know how to get in touch with me. If I want to get in touch with you, I'll let Sarah know. I need to go now and get another hour of sleep. Nice talking with you.

Goodbye," I said and hung up. I'm quite sure that he was normally the one who decided when a conversation would end.

I thought that I would not go back to sleep, but strangely enough, I dropped right off and slept from about four thirty to six thirty and awakened very refreshed. The phone call seemed like a dream, so I checked the phone and I had received a call from an unknown number at 3:27 that lasted until almost 4:30. Now what? I wondered.

I got up and did a four-mile walk and run. I learned that I needed to do that more often. I was dead on my feet when I got back. I grabbed a quick breakfast and coffee and headed over to the church for a nine o'clock staff meeting. As executive pastor, it was my option to chair the meeting. For the time being, however, I had deferred to the senior pastor in order to keep the transition smooth. There may come a time when that would change, but for now this was working well. We had a short time of visiting and catching up. The senior pastor then called the meeting to order. The meeting went smoothly and was over in less than an hour. After that, I met with the senior pastor to review anything that he felt I should see. About the only thing that I did not allow him to do unsupervised was the hiring and firing of staff. I trusted my own "nose" more than anyone else's when it came to hiring especially. It was easier to hire someone than to let them go. so it seemed important to make the best decisions on the hiring side so as to keep the need for letting people go to a minimum.

By the time my meeting with the senior pastor was over, it was almost lunchtime. I needed a couple of things, including a new suit. I drove out to the mall to do some shopping, which was not among my favorite things to do. I considered shopping a necessary evil. I visited a couple of men's clothing stores and found a nice navy blue suit with gray pinstripes at the second one. The sales associate told me that they were running a special and I could get a second suit for half price. I had been wanting a lightweight summer suit in a more casual color. I found one in a light tan that I really liked, so I bought two.

As I left, I noticed that I was hungry. I stopped at the food court and grabbed a salad and a sandwich and was enjoying a quick lunch when Sarah Harris walked up to my table. She was more friendly than she had ever been, so I invited her to sit down. She had a tray of food, so it was apparent that she was intending to have lunch. We chatted as we ate our lunch.

I told her how happy I was that she was attending our church. She smiled at me and said, "You don't have to keep up pretenses. I heard from my bosses that you spoke with them and that you are going to give me a message if you want to speak with them. Here's my number in case you need to contact me." She pushed a business card across the table. I looked at it. It said Sarah Harris, Financial Consultant, with a business address and a phone number. She had written another number on it.

I replied, "Thanks. I was not pretending, though. I really am pleased that you are attending the services for whatever reason."

She smiled a really bright smile at me and said, "You have really made an impression on the people that I work for. They are very afraid of you, but they respect you, and the funny part is that they really like you. Even when you know the person that you are talking to is an enemy, you are so pleasant to them. The idea of taking the two operatives in Michigan fishing with you and having them stay in your house was brilliant."

She laughed right out loud. "What were you thinking?"

"Well," I replied, "I figured that if they wanted to watch me, they could do so in relative comfort and I could keep an eye on them without having to change my plans. It was really convenient for me and coincidentally for them as well. Basically I would say that I did that primarily for myself. I was up there to go fishing. Besides, they looked so uncomfortable sleeping in their car."

She laughed again and said, "They reported that you are a really good cook as well. But the way that you disposed of them and the operative in Houston and then figured out who I am, is pretty impressive. We have never encountered somebody, in your position, with the field experience and savvy that you have."

I replied, "You flatter me or you have been operating in the shallow water. I don't know which." I wasn't going to tell her that I had swum with some big fish in my day and you had better be ready for the sharks because they would be there. Instead I just smiled at her.

She looked at me and shook her head. "That smile is so deceptive because it looks so genuine but covers a viper," she said.

"I hate snakes," I said with disgust. "You could call me almost anything, but a snake. That just gives me chills. I am not a snake, but I will defend myself. Know this, though, my intentions are never evil. I only intend to protect myself and the people who are depending on me. I would never do hurt just for the sake of hurting someone or venting my feelings." I continued, "I very much regret that those two boys are in jail, but they had orders to kill me. They are paying the price for thinking that I am ignorant and blind. That simply is not the case."

She replied seriously, "No, it is not. I wish they would just leave you alone. You are a really nice man."

It was my turn to chuckle. "Don't get all soft on me. I can't afford to lower my guard. I plan to live to be a hundred and run a marathon on my hundredth birthday."

Again she laughed. "I wasn't trying to do that. Those are truly my feelings. They had me thinking that you were some kind of brute. How else could you so easily handle some our best operatives? It just isn't true. You are kind, thoughtful, funny, and very sincere. But you do have a devious mind. Changing rooms like you did was brilliant. They never saw that coming. They thought they had killed you. When you confronted them in the parking lot, they were disarmed by their own astonishment."

"Well," I responded, "that was part of the strategy."

She nodded. "It worked, and that's a fact. Look, I need to get back to the office. You know how to get in touch. They are thinking about your offer, by the way." We said our goodbyes and each went our separate ways. I picked up a couple of items and headed back to the office.

CHAPTER 18

As I headed back to the office, it suddenly occurred to me that I had no idea how to get down to the boathouse that my fishermen friends had told me was on that little inlet. I decided to drive along the river and see if I could find it. I was below Stone House, so I drove down to the river and looked for a road or two tracks that went down by the river below the house. I could not find anything down river. I stopped an older gentleman that I saw walking up the street. "Excuse me, sir," I started, "do you live in this neighborhood?"

"All my life," he replied.

"Do you know of a road that goes along the river below that big house up there?"

"Why do you want to know?" he asked.

"I own the house and was told that there is a boathouse down there. I just don't know how to get to it," I replied.

He said, "There's not a road from this side. Maybe you can find a way from the upriver side. I never checked. I didn't even know there was a boathouse down there. Nobody ever goes down there that I know of."

"Thanks, I appreciate your help," I said.

"Don't guess I was much help, but you're welcome." He smiled.

I made a big circle and started looking on the upriver side. Over there, I could not find any street that went down along the river, either. I finally saw at the end of one of the streets what looked like it had been a narrow, weed choked alley. I drove very slowly down the alley, since it led in the right direction. I came to a turnaround with a locked gate and a sign that said, "Private Property of Stone House. No trespassing." I had my keys with me, so I started trying all of the keys on the ring that looked like padlock keys. On about the fifth key, the lock grudgingly gave, and I opened the gate. I decided to walk the rest of the way, not knowing whether there would be a place to turn around. I walked down to the river and then turned downriver along the edge.

There was a small path with uncertain footing. This was not the river proper, but the inlet that I had seen from the river side. I came to a strong fence that did not have a gate in it. The brush was too thick to work up and down the fence to try to find an opening. It appeared that the only access to the base of the cliff was from the river. I found that a bit intriguing. Moving a bit closer to the edge so that I could see over it, I noticed a steel ladder that was fastened into the side of the cliff. I debated as to whether I should try it and decided to do so. I called my office and asked Jennifer to check with me in an hour and if she could not raise me on the phone to call 911 and send them over here. She was more than a little bit freaked out, but I told her that it was no big deal and that I was on the property. I then mounted the ladder and started down.

The ladder felt solid enough, so I made my way to the bottom of the ladder and found a narrow trail leading along the bank of the inlet. I walked very carefully, as I did not want to meet up with a copperhead or rattlesnake along that narrow trail. I wasn't exactly "afraid" of snakes, but I did intensely dislike them. I arrived at the end of the trail after about five minutes of careful walking. There was a small set of stairs leading down to the face of the cliff. When I got down there, I noted two doors in the base of the cliff. One was for a boat to enter via a channel, and the other was an entry door for those of us who were afoot. The only lock was a cipher lock. There was no place for a key to open the door. I pondered how I was going to find the code to get into the boathouse. I noted a sign above the door. It said, "Here I come to fish and swim and sometimes sing my Favorite Hymns." I thought that odd, but couldn't make any sense of it rather than stating Doc's philosophy of recreation. I climbed back up the ladder and returned to the office. I was sure to let Jennifer know that she did not need to call me, as I was fine.

When I sat down at my desk, it was around three in the afternoon. I went over the mail to see if there was anything that required my attention, and there was not. I'm not particularly fond of writing letters. I personally preferred phone conversations. They were quicker in that you could pose a question, clarify the issues, and often have the answer in a matter of a few minutes. E-mail was also okay, although quite overrated in my view as well. Snail mail, as it is called, was my least favorite medium of communication, but at times it was necessary. I was pleased that there was no correspondence that required my response. I reviewed the mail and put a check mark in the corner so Jennifer would know that she could file it or dispose of it, whichever would be her preference, and move on.

My mind returned to the cipher lock on the boathouse. I wondered if there were another way to get inside besides the doors. I also wondered if the door on the boat channel had a remote control so that it could be open from the outside. After thinking about it, I came to the opinion that, if there was a remote control, it was probably on the boat and not "floating" around the place. Doc was quite methodical. He would have left in on the boat or in the boathouse somewhere. As I was thinking along these lines, I was sort of pacing the floor, but in a wandering-around-looking-at-things sort of way. As I scanned the books in the library rather absentmindedly, my eyes fell on a book entitled *Favorite Hymns*. I pulled it off the shelf. It was an older hymn book. As I leafed through it, I noticed that some of the hymns were marked. The markings were dated. It looked like about thirty of the hymns were marked. It occurred to me that maybe this was how Doc kept track of the code to the cipher lock. I remembered the rhyme on the door of the boathouse had mentioned singing "favorites." That explained why Doc had capitalized the *F* and *H* in *Favorite Hymns*. He had been leaving me a message even with that.

I checked the dates on the marked hymns and noted that the most recent ones were dated about two months before Doc's passing. They were 18 and 81. I thought that odd, but rather easy to remember. I chuckled at the simple yet almost undecipherable system he had devised to keep track of his code. I would have never thought of looking for the answer in that old hymnbook had my eye not fallen on it while puzzling over the code. The man was a surefire fox when it came to devising devious ways of hiding information without risking the loss of it. I spent a few moments remembering Doc as I thought of his brilliant mind. The world didn't know it, but it would never be the same without him.

I took a few phone calls and made a couple more. Jennifer came in and told me that she was leaving for the day. On impulse I asked her if she knew anything about the boathouse. I saw a guarded look in her eyes. She then advised that she knew about it, but had never been down there. She said that it was a very tough climb to get down there. I asked her how Doc managed to get there to go fishing in his later years. She looked rather surprised and asked me how I knew about that. I told her that I had run into some of his acquaintances and they told me about the boathouse and his love of fishing even until just a couple of years back. She just shrugged as though it was not important and said good night. I let it go, since it seemed that she did not want to talk about it. I would figure it out in due time. This exchanged cemented in my mind that there was something that I wanted to follow up on here.

As it was late in the afternoon, I decided not to take a shot at the boathouse this afternoon. I would do it soon, though, if only for my own satisfaction. I was not even sure there was a boat in there, but if so, it would be nice to have use of it. I could get up and down the river much faster in a power boat than I could in my canoe. I fully intended to check out the boathouse, but it would be several weeks before the thought even crossed my mind again. Tomorrow was going to begin a very busy time for me, but I did not know that yet. I ate a relaxed dinner, watched some news on TV, and retired sometime between eleven in the evening and midnight.

CHAPTER 19

Once again the phone was ringing in the middle of the night. My first thought was that Xavier was calling again, but when I answered it, the voice was female and hysterical. "Pastor Jack?" the voice said.

"Yes, I am," I responded.

"My husband has collapsed in the bathroom and is not responding to me!" she almost screamed.

"Who is calling, please?" I asked, trying to remain calm and keep the person on the other end calm as well.

"Oh, sorry," she said. "This is Joyce Snyder."

I heard real stress in her voice. "Tell me what is going on," I said.

She replied, "I got up about ten minutes ago, and Jerry was not in bed, which is not unusual. I went into the bathroom and found him lying on the floor with a cut on his head. I tried to wake him up, but he will not respond!"

"Did you call 911?" I asked.

"Yes, an ambulance is on the way," she responded.

"Joyce, I will be right over. Give me ten minutes."

"Oh, thank you!" she said and began sobbing hard.

"Hang in there. I'll be over as soon as I can."

As the Snyders lived just a couple of blocks from the church, I was there in just under ten minutes. I even took time to brush my teeth. When I arrived, the ambulance was coming up the street as well. I went in and found Joyce still in the bathroom trying to wake her husband. I helped her up and gave the paramedics room to work. From what I could see, there was not going to be much for them to do. It looked like I had just lost my senior pastor. I drove Joyce to the hospital following the ambulance. She wanted to ride in the ambulance, but the driver gave me a look and a very slight shake of his head, which led me to believe that he would rather that she not be in there. I quickly stepped in and told her that I would drive her and that we would be right behind the ambulance. She didn't like it very well, but agreed.

On the way to the hospital, she was very quiet. I could hear occasional sobs like little hiccups. Other than that, there was not conversation. When we arrived at the hospital, I walked around the car and helped her out. It was then that I noticed that she had not dressed. She was wearing a heavy robe.

"Is there somebody that I can call for you?" I asked.

She responded, "I need to call the children. Since they don't really know you, it would be better if I did it."

I replied, "I will do it, if you would like, but you need to do whatever you think is best."

She started calling her children. She told them that we were at Fairmont Hospital and that we really didn't know anything yet. One by one she told her four children how she had found their dad on the bathroom floor. With each one there was some variation of "I don't know yet, but it doesn't look good. I was not able to get any response from him. I don't think he was breathing, but I was so distraught, I don't really know."

We had been sitting for about fifty minutes more when the doctor came out to us. He had a serious look on his face. He said, "We did everything that we could to revive him, but he was gone. His brain had been without oxygen for too long. I am so sorry."

Joyce collapsed to the floor. I helped her up and nearly had to carry her to one of the nearby seats. There were a couple of recliners in the waiting room. I got her into one of them and then got some water to bathe her face. She soon opened her eyes and looked at me. "Why would God do this to us?" she asked.

I looked sadly into her eyes and responded, "I cannot begin to assume that I understand the workings of an all-wise God. I do know, however, that he does all things well. I'm not sure how that works, but I am sure that it's true."

She smiled a sad smile. "You sound like my husband. That is what he would say."

I felt tears burning my eyes. "Thank you," I said. "That is nice to hear."

Her family started arriving, and they started trying to comfort each other. I stayed in the background, keeping myself available but trying to respect their need for privacy and giving them room to grieve.

When I finally arrived back home, it was around nine thirty in the morning. I had not slept much last night, but had some work to do. Arrangements had to be made for a funeral. I had told the family that the church would be available for the funeral and all of the staff would be instructed to do whatever they could to help. Jennifer had already heard, so we took a few minutes to discuss what the process would be for his replacement. She told me that Doc had always reserved the right to make hiring decisions himself. He had certainly listened to input from others, but made the decision himself. That seemed like a good idea to me, so I told Jennifer that we would follow that model. We worked up an announcement to send out to announce the opening. We decided to hold the interviews after the funeral was over. So with the process in motion, I sat down to relax for a few minutes.

The phone awakened me. I had been sleeping for about a half hour. The voice on the other end was the oldest Snyder son. He seemed a bit nervous. I said, "How can I be of help, Bill?"

"Well, we were talking about the funeral and wondered if you would be very offended if we wanted somebody else besides you to have the funeral?" he asked.

I replied, "I would not be offended in any way. You do whatever it is that you need to do. Our facilities and staff are available to help in any way." In a way, it would be a relief if I did not have to have the funeral. I did not know Pastor Snyder very well. We weren't even really on a first name basis yet. Bill thanked me, and we said our goodbyes.

The funeral was huge. Not as large as Doc's, but very big. I saw a lot of old friends and friendly acquaintances. The dinner after the funeral was held in our fellowship hall. There was literally a ton of food there. Anybody who left there hungry had nobody to blame but himself or herself. During the lunch, I chatted with several old friends. Somehow the subject came up of holding a Bible conference at Stone Church in the fall. As we discussed it, the idea seemed to appeal to me more and more. I had wondered why we hadn't done something like this before. I was told that Doc had wanted to, but Pastor Snyder had opposed the idea. Doc had deferred to his point of view as the project would put a heavier load on the senior pastor. As I looked around the table, I realized that there were about six or eight excellent candidates for the senior pastor's position right here at this table. That was something to think about, since I had to think about it anyway. I asked all of them for their cards so that I would know how to get in touch with them ostensibly regarding the Bible conference, but secretly thinking that even if they did not apply, I should give consideration to each of them for the vacancy.

A couple of days after the funeral, the résumés started pouring in. They came in from all across the USA and other countries. I reviewed résumés until I thought my head would burst. There was no big rush, we had plenty of preachers on staff and had already set up an interim schedule for preaching. Also, the board had given the former pastor's widow a month to get moved out of the house. We would then need to clean and paint before moving a new pastor in. It seemed that we were looking at two to three months before this matter would be settled. We had discussed in the board how we would proceed. We were all reviewing résumés and would come together to discuss them. We were hoping that we could narrow the choices down to a dozen or less for the interview phase. We were asking them to send DVDs of their preaching so that we might observe them in action. We still reserved the right to call some to visit and preach for us. Some of them had quite a body of work available for review. Others did not have as much. We were early in the process and were not at all sure what we were going to do.

Sarah Harris had attended the senior pastor's funeral, which was in no way surprising. We spoke briefly following the service, and she had been curious about the process of selecting a replacement. I had explained that we had a system in place to make the transition and replacement as simple and painless as it could be. What I did not tell her is that the ultimate decision was mine as I was the owner of the property and the executive pastor of the church. Since I had no intentions of exercising that authority, it seemed pointless to discuss. Besides that, it was not any of her business. I had learned long ago that less information may cause speculation, but speculation was preferable to interference. It had caused me to ponder whether or not my newfound not friend might try to slip in a plant. It seemed logical that they might try that.

I would have to be on guard. It bugged me that I was becoming so suspicious of people, but they had done nothing to assuage the feeling that I needed to be on guard. The odd thing was that I had met a few priests who I believed to be more servants of God rather than servants of the church. Admittedly there weren't that many, but they did exist.

I leaned back from my desk and rested my head against the headrest on the office chair. I felt that I had read about all that I could, so I decided to listen to a sermon or two from some of the more interesting candidates. I opened one of the résumés that I had flagged and looked over it again. The gentleman's name was Riley Baker. He was pastor of a fairly good-sized church in Pensacola, Florida. I had, in fact, visited his church once, but had not preached that day. I opened the attachments and selected the DVD. As it opened, a trio was singing a special number in song. After the song was finished, Riley Baker stepped forward to begin preaching. Checking the time remaining on the DVD, I noted that the message was about thirty-nine minutes long. He read his Scripture lesson and started. When I awakened, it noted that the sermon had ended a half hour before. That didn't really speak too well for Riley, but it was not entirely his fault. I would withhold judgment and see if anybody else brought his name up.

Trying one more, I opened a résumé of a pastor from Northern California by the name of Mark Sparks. Now he grabbed my attention and held it through a very well-delivered message of nearly an hour on the Sermon on the Mount. I liked his preaching and delivery, so I put his résumé in a folder that would preserve it for further scrutiny. I then decided that it was time for some dinner. I didn't feel like making anything, so I headed to a nearby restaurant and grabbed a bite to eat.

Since I had taken an unscheduled nap, I felt quite refreshed as evening came on. I decided to go for a walk through town before heading back to the house. The restaurant where I had eaten dinner was near a mall, so I walked over to the mall and did some window shopping. As I was approaching the food court, I noticed Sarah Harris walking toward the tables with a drink in her hand. I was about to wave to her when she sat down at a table with a man. I looked at him. It was the tall, thin priest that I had seen with Stephen Lucas the day I was shot at back a few months ago. I did not make myself known, but grabbed a cup of coffee and sat down some distance away. As I watched, the priest reached into his briefcase and pulled out a sheaf of papers. It looked like he had several files with him. He put them on the table, and they began reviewing them together and discussing them. As they talked, they would take a file and shake their heads and put it in a stack. With others, they would nod their heads as though they liked what they saw and put those in a different stack. The approved stack was much smaller than the disapproved stack. I was quite curious, but did not approach them. After finishing my coffee, I slipped away and headed home. I couldn't help but wonder what they might have been doing there. It seemed a bit cloak and dagger to me, but what do I know?

When I got home, I watched another sermon, which I found mildly interesting. Then I watched some news on TV and went to bed. I was tired and wanted to get some sleep. I had a meeting with the church board tomorrow morning. It could be a long one. I didn't know.

The singing birds brought me back to the land of the living at daylight. Their songs were lovely, but their timing was horrible. After starting the coffee pot, I hit the shower and then sat down with a cup of coffee to start getting ready for the day. I had a meeting with the church board at ten and did not have any recommendations for people that I wanted to interview. I decided that I would try to look at a couple more before the meeting and then, if nothing popped for me, just go and see what they had.

I sat at my desk with a cup of coffee and started looking through e-mails again. There were three new ones in a cluster. I looked at them, and really nothing caught my interest. I did, however, jot down their names and gave their résumés a quick review. Looking over some of the other résumés, I noted some who had known Doc Lucas and studied under him. They might be worth a closer look. I copied a couple of the résumés that looked somewhat promising and put them in the folder that I was going to carry to the meeting. I had about an hour before the meeting, so I opened the preaching DVD. I watched the first twenty or so minutes of the DVD and turned it off. Everything the man said was good, and theologically he seemed to be right on the money. There was something about him that didn't feel authentic, though. I was reminded of something that Charles Spurgeon said regarding this type of thing. He said, "Discernment is not knowing the difference between right and wrong; it is knowing the difference between right and almost right." Something about this guy did not feel right. I selected the DVD from one of the other new applicants and got the same "vibe" from him. I looked at my watch and saw that I had ten minutes to get my stuff together and get over to the church, so I packed up to go.

When I walked into the meeting, there was a buzz of conversation. I sat down and waited for the chatter to subside before bringing the meeting to order. As the senior pastor was no longer with us, it was my duty to chair the meeting. We took care of the preliminaries, and I asked for old business of which there was none mentioned. Under new business, it was decided that the church would foot the bill for moving the senior pastor's widow to their retirement home, which they had built nearby. Then we started talking about a replacement at the senior pastor position. Several of the members had individuals that they wanted to discuss. I asked if they wanted to recommend them or just discuss them. Nobody was at the point that they wanted to actually make a recommendation. We spent the next two hours discussing the characteristics of some of the candidates.

One of the persons under discussion was among those new ones that had come in this morning. I made a note to have a chat with James Butler, who had brought the name to us. As it was well past lunchtime, I asked if there was any further business and then dismissed the meeting. We agreed that we would meet at the same time the following week. We also agreed that we would make more of an effort to present names that we could actually begin vetting. I encouraged the board to pray much about the decision. I was rewarded with several nods and a couple of rather dark looks. James Butler looked at me out of the corner of his eyes, but quickly looked away when he saw me looking his way. I found that a matter to ponder. A week later, I had further reason to ponder that look.

CHAPTER 20

The next morning, putting other matters aside, I concentrated on reviewing résumés, watching DVDs, and making notes regarding the various candidates. There was something about the three that had come in the morning of the meeting that disturbed me, but I couldn't really put my finger on it. I spent a couple of days really reviewing the candidates' presentations. I was scheduled to preach Sunday morning, so about Friday afternoon, I shifted gears and started working on a message for Sunday morning. As we were in transition, I hoped to bring something encouraging about finding the *right* senior pastor or something like that. Friday and Saturday passed quickly, and I found myself in church on Sunday morning. After the service, I greeted people as was the custom. As the crowd thinned out, I needed to get to a bathroom, so I walked down the hall toward the public restrooms even though I had a private one in my offices. This was closer. As I walked down the hall, I saw James Butler and Sarah Harris in what appeared to be intense conversation. They did not see me, and I suddenly felt like I should not disturb them. I went into the restroom. When I came out, they were still there. The sound of the door caught their attention. Sarah smiled and waved, but James looked like I had caught him peeking into the girls' locker room or something like that. I walked over and greeted them. We chatted for a few minutes about nothing in particular and then I headed out. They were walking out of the church as I mounted the steps to Stone House. They were still talking about something. James was waving his hands and acting like he was agitated by something.

I went home and had some lunch. After lunch, I sat down in my recliner thinking that I would do some reading. That turned out to be an unfulfilled hope. Two hours later, I was waking up from a long and wonderful nap. I had not even opened the book that I was planning to read. The book was on discernment, and I really felt the need to review some of those principles under the present circumstances. I started reading, as the book was not very thick. I got about halfway through it and felt the need for something to drink, so I went to the fridge and grabbed a soda. Almost on a whim, I sent the e-mail that had brought the three résumés that were bugging me to a friend of mine that was a computer guru. I requested that he find out from where they had been sent. I seemed a bit curious that three would come from what appeared to be the same place. I also decided that I would check their references and training records carefully before out next meeting.

We had an evening devotional at six and I wanted to finish the book before going, so I sat down and read through the rest of the book. I then put on some shoes and headed back over to Stone Church for the evening devotional. I was not responsible for it, so I could relax and enjoy. The service was brief and inspirational, which is a nice combination. I was back home by seven fifteen. Checking my e-mail, I found a response from my computer guru friend. He said that the three had been sent from a computer right here in town. It was located in one of the downtown office buildings, and he gave me the address. I sent him an e-mail thanking him for his help and telling him that it could have waited until Monday. He responded that it was no problem, he was on the computer anyway, which he usually was.

Since it was still early in the evening, I tucked the address in my shirt pocket and decided to drive downtown to see if I could figure out which business sent the résumés to me. The address was 407 W. Greenway. I punched the address into my GPS and started following the directions given. When I arrived at the location, I noted that there were two businesses in the building. One was All American Financial Services and the other was Monongahela Mortgage Services. It occurred to me that Sarah Harris had told me that she worked in a financial services office. It would be good to stop by to see if this was the place where she worked. If so, that explained some things, but left me still quite in the dark regarding many things.

The next morning, I arose to my regular Monday routine. I was at my desk by seven thirty and was doing some paperwork. At around nine, I remembered the address and jumped into my car to drive back to 407 W. Greenway. I pulled into the parking area and walked into the building. As I entered, I saw Sarah Harris walking into an office down the hall. I had what I needed, so I turned around and left the office. It was fairly certain that Sarah or someone working with her had sent those three résumés to us. I decided to check the other e-mails to see where they had come from as well. It was clear that those three candidates at least were ringers. It made me wonder how many others were and how we could change our process to protect ourselves from inadvertently hiring someone who was being run by an outside source. It had never crossed my mind that this would be a problem. Doc would have anticipated such a thing, but I had not.

After giving it careful thought, which I had been doing for several days, I decided to change the tack. The board would only consider résumés that I submit to them. This would no doubt be greeted with some discussion and possible dissension, but I was prepared to face that. I would introduce it at the next meeting, which would be Tuesday, which was tomorrow.

I spent the rest of the day at my desk studying and writing some letters. Correspondence was not my favorite way to spend a day, but it had to be done. At around three thirty in the afternoon, I had a sudden urge to go fishing. I told Jennifer that I would be out for the rest of the afternoon, changed clothes, and headed for the river. I put my canoe into the river and paddled up the stream a bit. I thought that I would try fishing the edge of the river and the drop-offs to see what I might find. I caught several fish, but nothing very big. There were a couple of keepers, but they weren't big ones.

As I fished, I noted that I was directly below Stone House. I was curious to see how Doc had entered the inlet into the boathouse. As I drifted slowly along, I suddenly got ahold of a big one. He didn't hit very hard, but he was really putting up a fight. I quickly dropped the anchor while holding the pole with my left hand. It took a good fifteen minutes to bring the fish to the boat on the light tackle that I was using. Now this was a nice one. It was a small mouth bass, and it measured right at nineteen inches. I put him on my stringer and started to pull the anchor up. As I was doing so, I glanced at the shoreline and noticed that the brush line along the shore was uneven. It was only noticeable if you were right close to it. From farther out in the river, it could not be seen. I weighed the anchor, secured the line, and started paddling toward the shore. As I did, I saw that there was a channel shaped like an *S* that was nearly invisible from out in the river because it entered on a downstream angle. It was about fifteen feet wide and wound into the place under the cliff where I knew that Doc's, now my, boathouse was located. None of it was visible from the river, it could only be seen from above or directly in front of the boathouse. It was quite cleverly concealed, if that were the intent.

I caught a couple of nice crappie in the channel and decided to add them to my catch. I then docked my canoe and went to the cipher lock that I had seen on my previous trip there. I punched in the number of Doc's favorite hymn. The second sequence opened the door. I stepped in, and to my great surprise, a video screen lit up and Doc's image and voice appeared. He said, "Congratulations, Jack. I knew that you would figure this out eventually. It really wasn't that complicated except that I never told you or anyone else that this place was here. In fact, my attorney didn't even know about it. If you don't have a few hours, you need to come back and do a walk through at a later date. Memorize the instructions that I am going to give you, because this recording will self-erase as soon as it has finished playing. I'm sure that you will find this an interesting place."

Then the instructions rolled, which were quite simple actually. I quickly jotted down the pertinent data and stuck it in my wallet. I checked out the boat. It was a beauty. A bass boat set up for fishing with all of Doc's best lures and equipment. He even left notes as to how to use them and when he would recommend each one. He always was thorough. I then checked out the other craft in there. It was a large and quite luxurious pontoon boat. It had all of the bells and whistles. It was apparently one of Doc's few concessions to luxury.

He had always been quite frugal, but everyone has their weaknesses. Bless his heart.

Very reluctantly I locked the place up and got back into my canoe and headed back out onto the river and upstream to where I had parked. I loaded my canoe and made my way back home. Once again, I had things to think about. And I had fish to clean. The good news is that freshly caught fish is the best, so I was quite certain that I would dine well this evening.

After I cleaned the fish, I put them in salt water to set for a couple of hours before cooking them. I decided that I would fry them. Although I rarely ate fried fish, it was my favorite way. I mixed up some cornmeal with some flour and spices. I then fried the fish in hot oil. They came out golden and crisp. I also did a microwave-baked potato and cooked some fresh asparagus. After throwing together a salad, I was ready to eat. It was delicious, and I ate too much. It's funny how eating too much can bring both guilt and great contentment. It was very satisfying, so the guilt did not prevail.

I sat down in my recliner to do some reading before bedtime, but my body had other ideas. The phone awakened me at around nine o'clock. As soon as I heard the voice on the other end of the phone, I knew who it was.

"Javier!" I said in genuine surprise. "What a surprise to hear from you at this time of the day. You usually call me in the middle of the night," I said laughingly.

"I know and apologize," he replied. "I am trying to be more thoughtful. I should not always awaken you to talk with you."

I didn't bother to tell him that he did anyway. "What's on your mind?" I asked.

"Well," he replied, "at the time of our last conversation, we left a few matters up in the air. Most importantly, I had asked for access to the journals that Dr. Lucas left in your care. Have you had the opportunity to review all of them yet?"

I replied, "No, I haven't completed my review of them. With my duties in a new environment, I have not had the opportunity to get them out and review them. Reading anything that Doc wrote requires focus. It's not something that can be done in leisure moments. I need to block out quality time to study his journals. So far, I haven't had time to do so."

He asked, "Have you reviewed any more than you had looked at prior to our last conversation?"

"Yes, I have, "I replied, "but only a couple more of the journals."

"How many are there?" he asked.

"I haven't counted them," I said. "There appears to be a dozen or more."

"How many have you read?" he asked.

I answered, "I have reviewed four or five of them to date."

He then shifted gears by saying, "The people that I work for will not be patient for long. They want to see what Dr. Lucas had figured out and what more he had theorized."

I replied, "From what I have seen in his journals, there was not much specific information in them. I'm not sure what he may or may not have known."

He said, "My superiors really want to know what you have. They will wait awhile longer, but they really are not very patient people. They are accustomed to being obeyed."

I replied, "If you are trying to threaten me, you are wasting your breath. I have had people shoot at me before both your people and others. I will do what I feel is the right thing. Your threats will not influence me either way."

He chuckled and said, "I already told them that, but they wanted me to call you. We'll talk again."

"Javier, before you go, I have a question for you," I said.

"What is it?" he asked.

"What is Stephen Lucas's role in this matter? How and why did you turn him against his father?"

"Well, why is pretty obvious, I think. As to how, we made him an offer that he could not resist," he replied.

I said, "I suppose to ask what that is would be a waste?"

He laughed right out loud and said, "You suppose correctly, until next time." The line went dead. Although on the surface, Javier's call had been very congenial, it somehow left me with an uneasy feeling. I thought that it was time to start taking more precautions. I needed to get to sleep as I had a meeting with the board tomorrow, and I was uncertain as to what, if any, opposition I would meet.

CHAPTER 21

When I walked into the conference room the next morning for the board meeting, all of the board members were already there. I took my place at the head of the table, and the formalities began. After the reading of the minutes of the previous meeting, I dropped my bomb on them. I cleared my throat and said, "I have an announcement to make." Everyone looked up from the papers or computer screens that they were looking at, looking at me with a question in their eyes. "Because of issues that I do not wish to discuss, I have decided that I am changing the process for replacing personnel from now on. Rather than reviewing the résumés as a group, I am going to review all of the résumés and vet the candidates myself. I will then bring to you the ones that are eligible."

I cautiously watched James Butler's face. He looked like he was about to go into shock. Somebody else saved him from having to say anything. Phil Sanders, who was in charge of children's ministries, said, "That is very sudden and seems extreme. I'm not sure that you can do that. We as a board have almost always made all of these decisions together."

I replied, "Tell me about the exceptions."

"Well," he replied, "on a few occasions, Doc Lucas would take things out of our hands. He never explained why he did it. It seemed heavy handed, but he was an old man and nobody would question him."

I replied, "You may question me, but I'm not going to promise you an answer. There are things that I can't explain to you."

Bill replied, "What if we won't stand for it?"

I dropped my head and thought for a couple of moments before replying. Finally I said, "I will accept the resignations of any who don't want to work here under these circumstances. Apart from that, I have nothing further to say on the subject. Please turn all of the résumés that you are holding over to me if you want them considered. Otherwise they will not be considered." James Butler looked like he had swallowed the world's largest dill pickle. He looked a bit sick really. Almost as an afterthought, I said, "Ask me any questions on this subject today; I will answer the best I can. After today, I don't want to discuss this again."

It was quiet for a few minutes before James Butler asked, "What brought you to such an extreme decision?"

I replied, "First of all, I don't consider this extreme. I am the sole owner of this church property and the executive pastor for as long as I desire to hold the position. To answer the question that you really want to ask, this is a precaution to ensure that we hire people who are part of our team and not part of another with strings outside of our ministry."

He looked hard at me. "Do you suspect that somebody is trying to infiltrate here?" he asked.

"Let's put it this way," I said, "Doc vested a lot of trust in all of us. For my part, I intend to keep the faith, so to speak. In keeping with that thought, I have made this decision. I have resources for vetting candidates that you don't have. This is the way it is going to be done. Any other questions?" There were none, so we moved on to other business.

I noticed that James was texting someone during the meeting and that he was visibly agitated. I decided to follow him once the meeting broke up and see who he met with, assuming that he thought his news was important enough to pass on and that he would not give details over the net. In order to not get caught up on a long conversation, I turned the meeting over to the vice chairman and left early. I walked quickly over to the garage and got Doc's Caddy out. It had not been driven for a while. I drove down the street and stopped out of sight of the driveway. After a few minutes, I saw James pull out in his white Jeep Cherokee. He turned left and started down the street. I waited until he made a turn and started down the street too. When I turned left, as he had, I saw his Jeep up ahead. I followed at a distance of about a block back. He made a right turn onto main street and parked. I was able to park up the street from him a few cars back. He sat in his car for several minutes. Then I saw Sarah Harris pull up in her car. He got out of his car and got into hers. They remained parked on main street. I could see that they were having a fairly heated discussion by the waving of the hands and the jerky movements of their heads. After a while, he got out of her car and walked back to his. He was clearly upset about something. She drove away, and he got into his car, but did not start it right away.

I decided to just walk into the restaurant and have some lunch. As I walked past James's car, I tapped on the window and smiled and waved at him and then headed into the restaurant. I motioned for him to join me. I found a booth, and a few minutes later, he walked in and joined me. He appeared to be nervous.

I said, "Order yourself some lunch; it's on me!"

He replied, "Oh, I don't know. I'm not very hungry. Maybe I'll have something light."

I thought those were rather nervous responses. The waitress came over, and we ordered. After watching James for a few minutes, I asked, "Is there something bothering you? You seem agitated or out of sorts somehow."

He dropped his head and sighed. "No, I'm fine," he replied.

"Okay," I said. "You seem uncomfortable or something."

When our food was brought, I bowed my head and prayed. When I finished praying and looked up, James had a hard stare fixed on me. When he saw that I noticed, he was flustered. "Well, let's dig in!" I said with enthusiasm and started to eat.

He took a bite and chewed slowly and thoughtfully. Finally he said, "How do you think the changes you have made are going to go over?"

I replied, "I honestly don't know. It depends, partially at least, on how well people work under authority."

"What do you mean?" he asked.

I replied, "Whether you like it or not, you all ultimately work for me. I happen to know that Doc pulled rank now and then."

He interrupted me with a quick, "You aren't Doc!"

"That is true," I said, fixing him with a level gaze, "and you all would do well to keep that in mind." I kept my voice soft and friendly when I said that, but it still had a strong impact on him.

He let out a long breath and said, "Wow! I was not expecting that!"

I replied, "It needed to be said, and now it's out there. I loved and respected Doc. In fact, he was my best friend. But I'm not him nor can I be. It would be a big mistake to try to figure out what he would do and try to do that. I just have to make decisions as I face problems and hope they work. If so, all will be well; if not, I'll be looking for lots more staff."

He grinned at me and said, "I guess you know the score, so play it out."

I replied once again very softly, "I fully intend to do just exactly that."

His eyes widened slightly, letting me know that he was taken aback by my directness. I dearly wanted to tell him to give my best to Sarah, but we went our separate ways without any more uncomfortable moments. It felt like there was a truce and an understanding between us. I was partially convinced that he did not understand Sarah's agenda. The jury was still out on that one, though.

When I got back to my office, Sarah was waiting for me. She just jumped right in, "You're a whole lot smarter than anyone in our organization realized."

I replied, "Thank you, I think, and nice to see you too."

She was disgruntled. "The time for niceties is past. Javier really is not going to like this. He thought that it would be fairly easy to slip a plant into your organization."

"Don't you mean that he really doesn't like it?" I asked. "You didn't come here to see me without talking with him first."

She responded, "He said that you would see right through me. How do you do it?"

I smiled at her. "That would be telling," I said.

"Javier said to tell you that the gloves will come off if we don't make progress very soon," she said.

I looked at her calmly and said, "Tell your boss that his high-handed tactics have not worked to date and will not. I am not afraid of him or his minions. This is not my first rodeo. If he wants to declare war, he should be aware that it's always a two-way street.

Some people shoot back. If he wants to play for keeps, I know how that game is played. I wonder if he does."

Sarah was visibly upset. "I can't tell him that! You don't know who you're dealing with!"

I looked her right in the eye and said, "Neither do you." I then stood to indicate that the conversation was over. She stood up but hesitated to leave. "What is it?" I asked.

She said, "You are really a nice person. I really don't want to see you get hurt, and I have seen what Javier does to people who get in his way. Be careful!"

I smiled at her with genuine pleasure. "I will do just exactly that, and thanks for the heads-up!" With that we parted company, and I thought that it was time to carefully explore that boathouse. I'm not even sure why that thought entered my mind, but there it was.

I went back to my office and finished up some paperwork. Then I drove to the end of the lane where the ladder went down the cliff to the boathouse. As I descended the ladder, I was pondering what surprises Doc had in store for me. I punched the code into the door and entered the boathouse. I then started up the stairs to see what I might find. The stairs were fairly long and wound up in a chamber that took me by surprise. There were computers and monitors. I noted that I could see nearly every room and angle in Stone House and Stone Church. As I explored the system, I also noted that there was audio, so I could, if I wished, listen in on conversations in the house and church. That was interesting. There was a door on the far side of the room that was locked. I tried the keys that had been given to me when I took over Stone House and Stone Church. None of them opened the door.

I sat back down and started looking through the house and church screen by screen. This was a very elaborate system. I saw the youth pastor and the worship leader were sequestered in the youth pastor's office, so I tuned in on the audio. They were talking about the meeting of this morning. They were not against it, but they were a bit confused by it. It was clear that they had no idea what was going on. I noticed somebody walk into one of the unused offices. It was Mary, one of the secretaries. What caught my attention was that she seemed a bit nervous and had moved into the room rather furtively. There was no reason that I knew of for her to be there, but neither was there any reason why she should not be there. The door opened and in walked Sarah Harris with James. Now they had my attention. I tuned to audio in and listened to their conversation.

James said to Mary, "We need your help on something."

Mary replied, "What do you mean?" She did look genuinely confused.

Sarah said, "We know what is going on between you and Brad." Brad was the youth pastor at Stone Church and a single gentleman.

Mary replied, "What do you mean? There is nothing going on between Brad and me!"

James replied, "We know that, but we'll make the case, if necessary."

Mary was stunned. "How can you do that? You're part of the pastoral staff!"

"True," he replied, "but we do what we must."

"What do you want me to do?" Mary asked.

Sarah spoke up, "We want to get rid of Pastor Jack. We feel he is heavy handed and authoritarian. The church should not be run the way he is going about it." That made me chuckle considering who her bosses were.

Mary replied, "What does that have to do with me?"

James replied, "We want to get him in a compromising situation. We want you to get him alone in a prearranged place and embrace him so we can get some pictures. We'll have a camera set up to get the pictures. Once that is done, we can doctor the photos to make them look worse than they are."

"I won't do it!" Mary said.

"If you don't, you are finished here," threatened James. I figured it was time for me to take a hand. I picked up my cell phone and punched James's number. I had input all of the staff phone numbers when I took over. I watched as James heard his phone ring. He looked to see who it was. "Speaking of the devil," he muttered and answered the phone. In pleasant voice said, "Pastor Jack, we were just discussing you!"

"I know," I replied. "You meet me in my office in fifteen minutes and don't be late. In fact, I suggest that you be there waiting when I arrive."

It was comical because I had seen this scene played out in so many movies. He stood there with his mouth open staring at the phone. Then he started blustering. "You don't even know whether or not I can get there in fifteen minutes!"

My response was, "The clock is ticking. You'd better get moving. See you in a few minutes."

He turned to Sarah and Mary with a shocked look on his face and said, "I think he can see us!"

"How do you know that?" asked Sarah.

"I don't know, but it's like he read my mind," replied James. "I have to meet him in his office in fifteen minutes. I'd better get going." He hurried out of the classroom leaving Sarah and Mary looking at each other. Without a word, Sarah turned and walked out of the room leaving Mary alone. She looked completely mystified but greatly relieved.

For my part, I looked at the computer system to see if the feeds were recorded. I found them and saved the file of the exchange that I had just seen in case it would be needed. I then e-mailed the file to my office computer. After that, I returned to the house and my office.

CHAPTER 22

I quickly returned to my office all the time thinking of that locked door in the office above the boathouse. How in the world was I going to get into that office? Good question, for which I had no answer available.

James was at my office waiting for me. I ushered him in, and we sat down. Although I did not like doing what had to be done, I had to confront him. The problem that I was having was that there had been no time to prepare for this. I did not like flying by the seat of my pants. Improvising in such matters was a risky policy. I breathed a prayer and launched into the subject.

"James, do you enjoy your job here?" I asked.

"I do very much like my job and the people with whom I work," he replied.

"Let's talk about loyalty for a few minutes," I said. He looked at me sharply but said nothing. "Did Doc demand loyalty?" I asked him.

His reply was revealing, if not surprising. "We never talked about it. It was just always assumed."

I changed tack on him. "When did you start seeing Sarah Harris?" I asked.

"Well, uh, what business is it of yours?" he blustered.

"Everything that goes on at Stone Church and everything that has to do with the personnel working here is my business," I replied. "Are you aware that I am the sole owner of Stone Church, Stone House, and all of the appertaining property as was Doc?" I asked him.

"Well, no, I was not aware of that information," he replied.

"That is the case, however," I announced.

"So, what are you saying?" he asked.

"I'm saying that you work for me and I have full authority to retain and discharge employees at my own discretion without having to answer to anyone. In fact, the church board answers to me, not the other way around. Do you understand that?" I asked him.

"I do understand that," he replied.

"Does that question about loyalty make any more sense now?" I asked.

"It does," he replied.

I moved on. "Are you aware of why Sarah Harris, not being a member of our church, takes such an interest in our ministry?" I asked.

"She said that she is a very concerned layperson who wants to make sure we get the right person to hold the senior pastor position," he replied.

"What did she give you or promise you to get you to propose names for her?" I asked.

He looked at me for a long moment before responding. "You are just suspicious by nature, aren't you?"

I laughed at that. "I wasn't until recently, but I'm getting that way," I replied.

"Where do you think she got those résumés that she asked you to support? Did you vet these guys before supporting them? What is her agenda?" I fired questions at him in rapid succession.

"I don't know the answers and, no, I did not vet them. She said that they were all very well-qualified candidates. She was afraid due to your inexperience that you would make a bad choice," he replied.

"I'm going to let you in on a little secret," I told him. "Sarah is not part of our church. In fact, I would bet that the people that she has recommended are all Jesuit-trained and are sent in as plants to work in protestant ministries while under the control of the Vatican."

He looked at me like I was nuts. "Now you're sounding just crazy! She is a nice lady, and she really loves the Lord," he said.

"I have spoken with her handler at the Vatican. She is a plant, and her intent is to sow confusion. That is why she had tried to exert influence over you. You need to wise up, James," I replied. "In fact, you need to decide whether you work for me or for them. It can't be both ways. I'm operating under the presumption that you did not understand what is going on here. For that reason, I'm willing to give you a chance to redeem yourself by going on a six-month probation. During that time, you will log every meeting with every person, both work-related and social. You will submit the log to Jennifer every Friday. If I find that you failed to log one meeting with anyone, you will be discharged. If you are not willing to meet these conditions, be off the property by the end of the workday today. You may not think about it. Make up your mind and give me an answer."

He stared at me with his mouth hanging open. "Are you serious?" he asked.

"As a heart attack," I replied.

"Okay, I'll stay. I don't want to lose my job. I really love it here," he said.

"Then you can start by logging this meeting and every meeting with everyone for the next six months. Encountering people in stores, etc., doesn't count. Don't try to fool me, though. It won't work," I told him.

He responded, "I believe you. In fact, I have no idea how you found about Sarah or figured out where those recommendations came from. You got yourself a deal and my thanks for not firing me outright. I'll be a team player from now on."

"That's what I want and need. Thanks, James," I said, offering him my hand. We shook hands, prayed together, and went our separate ways. I was glad that I did not have to reveal to him that Doc had planted cameras all over the property.

It was too late to go back to the boathouse today, so I went back over to the house. It had been an eventful day, and I was worn out. I figured that I would be hearing from Sarah or Javier soon. I didn't want to talk with either one of them. I checked in with Jennifer. There was nothing pressing, so I checked out for the day. Before going to bed, I turned my cell phone off.

CHAPTER 23

The next morning, I was at my desk with a cup of coffee at around six. There was some personal mail from yesterday that Jennifer had not opened but placed on my desk. I opened the top drawer of my desk to grab my letter opener, but it was not in the tray where it normally was. I reached back into the drawer and found it. As I was removing my hand from the drawer, I felt an irregularity with the back of my hand on the top of the drawer, which was the bottom of the desktop. I reached in and felt and found something was taped to the bottom of the desktop. I peeled the tape off and pulled out a key. I immediately knew what door the key would open. I was headed for the boathouse again.

I told Jennifer that I would be out most of the morning but would be available via cell phone, and headed back to the boathouse. After climbing the stairs, I quickly tried the key in the locked door, and it opened immediately. Looking around, I found that I was in a small room with an exact replica of the fireplace in my office against what would most likely be the wall that would adjoin the office. I was both mystified and intrigued with what I was seeing. There were some locked file cabinets in the room. I tried the keys on my ring, and they opened. In them were more of Doc's journals.

He had not trusted some of his research to his computer. He had taken no chances on leaking anything even accidently. One thing that was noticeable in the room was that it was clean and recently dusted. The smell of a dusting chemical was in the air. Somebody knew about this place, and I was betting that it was Jennifer.

I focused my attention on the fireplace. It was exactly like the one in my office down to the smallest detail. As I pondered that fact, I examined it closely. I could see no visible difference. One would have to examine them side by side to note any difference. I decided that I would say nothing to Jennifer about this for the time being. I needed to figure this out. I had my suspicions, but was not able to put my finger on what was going on here.

Opening the file cabinets, I began to review what Doc had put in these reports. I found that he had proof that several cloning projects were going on. It was clear that the project for cloning Jesus was several generations old. There were also projects to clone other dead people. Doc was convinced that the number 666 in the book of Revelation was the number of the clone that would actually become the antichrist. Doc also thought that there might be some efforts to clone King David, but to what end, he did not speculate. He also thought there might be efforts to clone other men of great intellect from the Greek and Roman period. It was fascinating to read the reports. He was convinced that cloning was a much more mature science than the official reports were leading the general public to believe. I suddenly noticed that my stomach was growling. I looked at my watch, and it was well past noon. I locked the files away and left locking the door behind me. I had another puzzle to unravel. Doc was that way. He was always constructing puzzles for people to solve. This was a ten out of ten.

As I made my way back to Stone House, I pondered what I had just discovered. There was much to sort out, and that was a fact. This all seemed so fantastic that it was making me feel like I was in the twilight zone. Yet I know what I had seen and experienced. That, at least, was real. The two questions that kept whirling around in my head were, "Where did all this lead and what was the meaning of two identical fireplaces?" I thought that I had a plausible, if outlandish, answer to the second question. Doc was an old man. He must have devised an entry from his office to his secret office without going through the boathouse. I'd have to figure out how that worked. The first question had my head spinning.

Arriving at the house, I made myself a sandwich and a salad and ate lunch. After lunch, I went into my office. There were some phone calls to return. One of the calls was from Sarah Harris. I returned that one last. She asked me to meet her at a local diner at around four in the afternoon for coffee. I agreed to do so, somewhat mystified. The rest of the afternoon was spent in writing letters and taking calls. There was really nothing of consequence. It was mainly routine work that had to be done. Some of it would drop off once we installed a new senior pastor.

At four in the afternoon, I walked into the diner and grabbed a table. After ordering coffee, I waited. A few minutes later, Sarah Harris walked in with a distinguished older gentleman. They came directly to the table where I was seated. I stood to receive them, and Sarah said, "Pastor Jack, meet my boss, Javier."

I was astounded, but covered well. Extending my hand, I said, "It's a pleasure to meet you after our phone conversations!"

He smiled and said, "I just wanted to put eyes on you. I have been very curious about you."

We held a firm handclasp, and I smiled at him and said, "What you see is what you get."

His reply was gently sarcastic. "Not hardly!" We both chuckled at that and sat down.

As I sat across from Javier, I gave him the once over. When he walked in, I had noted that he stood around six feet two inches tall. He was slim with a very erect bearing. He moved with a grace that belied his years. He looked to around seventy years of age, but moved like a man much younger. My suspicion was that he had years of martial arts training behind him, which tended to keep an older person more graceful as they aged. His face was lined, and he spoke English with a distinct Spanish accent. He said something to Sarah in Spanish, maybe thinking that I would not understand. What he said translated to "If we can work with this guy, good. If not, we'll have to take care of him." He apparently was not aware of the fact that I was fluent in Spanish. I chose not to react or display any indication that I had understood.

"Javier," I began. "To what do I owe the pleasure of a visit from such a distinguished member of the Vatican staff?"

He looked at me sharply to determine whether or not I was being sarcastic. He apparently decided that I was not. "Well," he began, "you have caused so much trouble for us that some thought that I should actually meet you and see what we are dealing with."

I replied, "I'm honored that you would come and visit, although I am aware that this is not a social visit. No doubt you travel with quite an entourage."

He smiled at that and asked me, "Can you identify my operatives here?"

I glanced around the room and picked the ones that I thought were probably his security people. I was about to identify them when I thought better of it. I purposely pointed out people who I was pretty sure were not and then picked a couple of the more obvious ones that I thought were his people. He looked at me and then chuckled. "You're not playing fair," he said.

"What do you mean?" I asked.

He said, "You're better than that, which tells me that you are trying to avoid tipping your hand and showing your skill. Very smart!" He gave me an appraising look and said, "There's much more to you than meets the eye. We have reviewed your military and work records and found nothing that would indicate the skill set that you demonstrate." I did not tell him that most of my military record had been manufactured to cover the work that I actually did. There was probably no official record of my training and assignments. The other side of that was that the unofficial records were buried so deeply that anyone presently at the Pentagon would probably have no idea where the records were or how to access them. Some things got buried and were meant to stay that way. He continued, "It makes me wonder how deep this well of spy craft and competency goes."

I replied, "I guess there is only one way to find out."

The waitress came over, and we ordered some food. When she walked away, Javier looked at me and said, "I sincerely hope that there is some way that we can work together."

I looked down at my hands and then looked him in the eye and replied, "I would have to know that we really have common interest. I don't intend to cooperate with you just to make it easy for you to watch me and manage the situation. In addition, if I am to give you access to Doc's research, you have to give me access to yours."

He studied my face and then sighed and said, "They told me that this would not be easy, but they had no idea that you would be so demanding."

I grinned at him and replied, "I don't consider it demanding to require a level playing field. There is no advantage in that; just an even chance."

"If you don't give us access to Doc's research, there are some at the Vatican who just want to get rid of you and have an end of it," he said.

Again I smiled at him and replied, "As you well know, that is easier said than done. Although I am not a violent man, I will defend my person."

Javier laughed out loud at that and said, "We have firsthand knowledge of your efficiency in doing that! I think that at my peak, I might have been able to take you, but not now. I'm not sure I ever would have been able to outthink you. Your moves to date have been brilliant. It almost seems like you knew what we were going to do next."

"Don't worry, you don't have a leak, as far as I know," I replied. "Self-preservation is a strong motivator."

"It is indeed," Javier replied.

Sarah, who had been listening without comment, piped up and asked, "How did you figure out what James and I were up to?"

I gave her a sharp look and said, "Some matters are better left unaddressed."

Anger flashed in her eyes as she replied sharply, "That's not fair! You read our minds and just walk away like it's no big deal!"

"I wouldn't say it's not a big deal," I replied. "I just don't intend to tell you how it happened. There's a difference."

She gave me the dagger look and huffed at me. "You're so secretive!" she grumped.

Javier said, "I too am curious as to how you figured out what they were up to."

"That's one that will remain a question mark," I said.

Just then our food arrived, and we began to eat after giving thanks to God for our food.

"Are you going to be around for the weekend?" I asked Javier.

"Maybe," he replied. "Why do you ask?"

"I thought you might enjoy speaking at my church," I said.

He looked at me with a clearly shocked expression on his face. "Why would you do that?" he asked.

"Haven't you ever spoken in a Protestant church before?" I asked.

"Well, yes, but I never thought that you would invite me to speak," he said.

"Well, I am asking you to do just exactly that. What do you say?" I asked.

He looked at me with a bemused expression on his face and said, "Okay, I'll do it!"

"Great," I responded, "I'll get it set up for you. Why don't you come for breakfast at around eight thirty and we'll make a morning of it."

"Agreed!" he said then he sat back in his seat and studied me. "You are full of surprises!" he exclaimed. "That is the last thing that I would have expected from you."

"The truth is that you don't really know me," I reminded him. "You just know about me." He gave me a rather long appraising look and said nothing else on the subject.

When we were finished eating, we chatted for a few minutes and headed our separate ways.

"Until Sunday!" I said as they walked away.

Javier replied, "Sunday!"

I contemplated what he might say to his bosses regarding the invitation to speak in my church. I drove back to Stone Church and arranged for the change in the schedule. Then I went to my office.

CHAPTER 24

On Saturday afternoon, I stopped by a local grocery store and picked up some fresh fruit along with eggs and milk. I had bacon and sausage in the freezer. Sunday dawned in fine fashion. The sun was bright and beautiful. Javier and Sarah showed up right on time, and we ate a hearty breakfast. As we chatted, Javier asked if he could see my office. I saw no reason why he should not, so I showed him in there after breakfast. We sat down and chatted. He expressed great admiration for Doc. He said that rarely had he met anyone with such a sharp intellect. I agreed with him on that.

"You're pretty sharp yourself," he said to me.

"The truth is that I'll never hold a candle to Doc," I replied. "He really knew how to think outside the box."

Javier smiled at me. "It is strange to see you behind that desk rather than Dr. Lucas."

I was a bit surprised but did not allow it to show. "So you visited him here while he was alive?" I asked.

"Yes, indeed," he said. "I tried hard to convince him to share information with us. He never did agree to do so, but never really said no either. He could do that better than most."

I chuckled as I responded, "Indeed he could. He was never devious, but often evasive."

Javier said, "That is well-put! It describes him to a *T.* I would often leave thinking that he had agreed with me, but then realize that he had committed to nothing. It really aggravated me. I was accustomed to being bested by anyone, let alone an old man." He looked at me with an amused look. "I guess my pride got the better of me."

"Well," I said. "He had a way of keeping me humble, I know that," I said. We both chuckled and then sat there for a few minutes in silence, each with his own thoughts.

I suddenly realized that Sarah wasn't with us. "Where is Sarah?" I asked him.

"She is cleaning up after breakfast while we chat," Javier said.

"She didn't need to do that," I said. "I have all afternoon to do that."

"I asked her to do it so that we could talk," said Javier. "I feel like we need to talk and try to come of an understanding."

"OK by me," I said. "What do you want to discuss?"

He gave me another of those appraising looks. He started, "You cannot believe how shocked I was when you called me by name. It's hard to believe that you could figure out my identity with no more information that is out there. Very few people would ever think to look at the graduates and look for those who were alive, but out of circulation. That was really a brilliant strategy. I can see why Dr. Lucas wanted you to carry on his work. I don't even know if he would have thought of that. It makes me wonder where you were trained and what in your background has been hidden or redacted."

I looked at him with a puzzled face and said, "What are you talking about?"

He replied, "We have searched everything that is available on you. We know every school you ever attended, your sports efforts, your friends and enemies, your military records, and there is nothing in your background to indicate the expertise and outright spy craft that you display. Your military record does not indicate anything that even comes close to this kind training. So my question to you is, what are we not seeing?"

I smiled at him. "Javier, you are seeing all there is to see."

He smiled a genuine smile at me and said, "Oh, I know that, but what I would like to know is, what is there that I cannot see?"

I winked at him and said, "If I told you that, I'd have to kill you."

At that, he laughed a real belly laugh and I laughed with him.

"Let's change the subject a bit," he said. "Do you think that we are going to be able to work together?"

I appeared to be thinking about it, but was really only doing it for effect. When I spoke, I said, "I would assume that at whatever level you expect me to share information that you are going to reciprocate?"

Javier did something that was a bit unexpected. He replied very honestly, "I don't think that will happen. My people are not accustomed to sharing information. They are accustomed to demanding and getting cooperation. They can get really rough if they don't get what they want. I really don't want to see you get hurt. You are a good man. A better man than I expected. I actually really like you as a person. I really regret that we're enemies."

I looked at him surprised with his candor and replied, "Just because we're adversaries doesn't mean that we have to be enemies. Let's not be enemies even though we can't help but be adversaries. How about that?"

He looked down and said, "I should never have come here. When I go home, I have to demonstrate hatred for you. That is going to be hard because I don't hate you. In fact, I have decidedly friendly feelings about you. I definitely admire and respect you. I don't know what to do."

I replied, "I wish I could help you. If the openness is not reciprocal, then you're just asking me to give everything with nothing in return. That is not going to happen. I don't want to be difficult, but if we're going to negotiate, we both have to give something to get something. If we aren't going to negotiate, then let's go to church."

He gave me a rueful look. "Let's do that."

Javier's address to the church was interesting. He mixed a lot of church history into his homily and weaved a fascinating message. At its foundation, the gospel is so simple and he kept it simple. He stayed away from controversial topics. He seemed surprised that our congregation was so receptive to him and his message. After the service, the ladies of the church had planned a church dinner. It was potluck, so there was a great variety of food available. We all did our best to do what was expected of us as we bellied up to the table. It was a feast, and feasting was expected.

I saw Javier was greeted by and engaged in conversation by a great number of our people. I noticed that Sarah was always hovering near. It occurred to me that she might be his handler rather than he being her boss. It seemed a bit absurd, but she seemed to be trying to eavesdrop on his conversation. I decided to throw a monkey wrench into her plans, so I slipped up and engaged her in conversation. It amused me that she seemed very anxious to get away from me, but didn't want to appear rude. As Javier drifted farther away, she became more and more agitated.

Finally I asked her outright, "Sarah, are you spying on Javier's conversations?"

She looked at me angrily. "Of course not!"

I gave her a piercing look. "You are reporting on him to someone. Does he know that?"

At first she started to be defiant, but then the defiance wilted. "No, he doesn't."

I asked her, "Is he actually your boss, or are you his handler?"

She responded, "He is my boss and my handler. Some people above both of us think he is getting soft on you and are not sure that he can be trusted anymore."

"Sarah, where is your loyalty?" I asked her.

She responded, "To the project. It is a marvelous idea that we may be able to bring about the second coming of Christ!" Then she stopped like she had said too much.

I said to her, "Sarah, I have already figured out what is happening. Nothing you have said is news to me. I saw the cloned children in Mexico and am aware that there are other 'orphanages' around the world where this is going on. I didn't even need confirmation, since I have seen it with my own eyes."

She looked really relieved. "I have to catch up with Javier! Where has he gone?"

I looked around, and he was not visible at the moment. I told her, "I'll check the men's room." When I walked in, he was washing his hands. "Sarah was worried about you because she could not see you," I told him.

Looking puzzled he asked, "Why should she worry about me?"

"Good question," I responded. "You might want an answer to that one."

He gave me a dark look and left the men's room. I was just a couple minutes behind him and found him in deep conversation with Sarah. He did not look like he was any too pleased with her. I felt satisfied that I had sowed some distrust in the camp of my adversaries and was not displeased with the thought.

A short time later, they came up to me and announced that they must be leaving. The tension between them was notable. We shook hands, and I extended an open invitation for him to visit when he could and if he would like. As they were taking their leave, I shook his hand and held it a moment longer than necessary.

"Watch yourself," I said with a warning look in my eyes. I don't think Sarah caught it because she was already walking out the door.

"Thanks," Javier responded, "you too." With that they were gone.

Although I very much liked him, I determined to have my office, house, and the church swept for bugs at the earliest possible time. I disliked even thinking that way, but trusting people in a situation like this was far too risky. I am not a person to take an unnecessary risk. This one was unnecessary. Sweeping for bugs would start tomorrow morning. I would have to check my clothes as well. Spying seemed to be a habit that they had developed over time. I knew that they had spied on me before and would not take the chance again.

On Monday morning, the technicians found bugs in my office, my quarters, Jennifer's office, the kitchen, the church office, sanctuary, and rest rooms. They checked the entire building and pronounced it clear of bugs by three thirty in the afternoon. I was surprised at how many they found in my quarters. It occurred to me that while Sarah was "cleaning up the kitchen," she was doing a few other things as well. I chalked it up to the cost of doing business. Having Javier speak in my pulpit turned out to be a rather expensive indulgence. Maybe that's why Doc never did it. There was always fallout from whatever one does. The fact of the matter is that we can choose our actions, but we cannot choose the consequences. Although there was no harm done, I would have to be more careful in the future. It made me wonder if Javier had made some contacts in my church that would net him information in the future. He was very persuasive.

CHAPTER 25

It was time to select a senior pastor. We had vetted many, interviewed a few, and now we had to make a decision. I sat down with the board and the assistant pastors and asked them to look over the three candidates who had made all the cuts and were still in consideration for the position. I reminded them that, if necessary, I could take the process out of their hands. What I asked them to do was write the name of one of the three candidates on a piece of paper and turn it in. If we had a strong majority, we would probably call that person as our first choice. If we were found to be divided, I would convene an executive committee to make the choice. We were only going to take one ballot. I stressed to them the importance of praying and keeping their vote between them and the Lord. I purposely had not revealed the names of the three candidates to anyone so that there could be no pre-vote electioneering. I wish that I did not believe that they would do that, but I was pretty sure that they would, so I tried to remove the possibility.

When I presented the three names, there was some grumbling about not having the opportunity to take time to pray over the three. I said, "It was my thought that a large part of the praying that was done might be done between board members rather than to the Lord. I'm afraid that some of you might seek more guidance from each other then would be healthy for the process."

The music minister shot back, "Don't you trust us?"

I replied softly, "Do you trust me? Do you trust each other? It's better this way; it will be a more pure process."

When the vote was in, there was a strong majority for one Michael Longstreet. He was a middle-aged pastor with lots of experience. His family was grown and out of the home. I picked up the phone in the conference room and put it on speaker. When Michael answered, I advised him that he was on speaker with the board of Stone Church.

"Michael," I said, "we have just voted overwhelmingly to call you as the senior pastor of Stone Church. Out of the final three candidates, you were a strong first. What do you say to that?"

Michael cleared his throat. "First of all, I am very pleased to hear that. May I ask what the vote tally was?"

I responded to that, "I'd rather not say. I prefer that you make your decision based on what God wants rather than how the vote went. It is really not important. We know how fickle people can be. This is a good board, but we are people just the same. I will tell you that I personally voted for you, if that helps."

There was a pause then Michael said, "I appreciate your candor. It puts me in an odd position, but I accept because the Lord has been indicating that this call would be coming. In fact, I stayed home today from an outing with the church because I felt this call would be coming. This confirms that it was the Lord leading and not my own feelings. I will need to give notice here and then make plans to move."

The board clapped and then I said to him, "I will send you a salary and benefits package by e-mail. Please review it and, if it is satisfactory, respond in the affirmative. If we need to engage in further negotiations, we will do so. Congratulations, Senior Pastor Longstreet, and welcome to the team!"

He replied, "Thank you, and thanks to you all. I'm sure we'll be communicating over next few days and weeks. I am really looking forward to working with you all. God bless!"

With that, we said our goodbyes and the call ended.

I looked around the board and smiled at them. "Are you pleased?" I asked. The consensus was that they were pleased to have the problem of a senior pastor solved. Several of them had been taking up the slack for the time that we had been without one. Their lives would certainly be easier. There were a few glum faces in the group. That was to be expected. The meeting adjourned, and we went about the business of the day.

After having some lunch, I went into my office and sat down to do some work. There were letters that needed my attention. It amazed me how many "ministries" petitioned local churches for funds to support their ministries. They were service organizations. They charged fees for their services, but also wanted churches that didn't even use their services to support them. I might be a jerk in some people's eyes, but I did not send money to organizations unless I personally knew the people behind the ministry and how they spent their money. Most of these didn't even dignify a response from me. If I responded, I told them that before our church would support them, I would personally visit their offices, interview their executives, and review their books to see how they spent their money. Most of them lost interest in our support upon receipt of that letter. There was a pile of those requests in the mail. I sent out my standard response. I returned a couple of phone calls, and the afternoon was gone. Jennifer popped in to say that she was leaving and the work day was over.

I decided to spend a couple of hours fishing, so upon leaving the office, I drove down to the boathouse. I entered the boathouse and prepared the fishing boat for use. After checking my gear, I opened the door and eased slowly out into the channel that led to the river. Since I had speed in my favor today, I cruised up river for a couple of miles until I saw a likely bend with several downed trees lying in the water. I shut down the power and used the electric trolling motor to maneuver the boat to where I wanted to fish.

After making several casts, I hooked into a nice bass. When I landed him, I noted he was a keeper and put him in the live well. I picked up a couple more and then saw a spot just up river from where I was. I quietly slipped up there using the trolling motor. On the first cast, I hooked a real fighter. It took a few minutes to land him. When I netted him, I noted that he was a big one. When I measured him, he was 21.5 inches long. I snapped a picture to send to my friend in Michigan. We had fished together for several years.

I noted that it was time to pack it in, so I put my poles away and fired up the motor to head back to Stone House. I had a smooth and uneventful ride back to the boathouse. I secured the boat, cleaned the fish, and dumped the "mess" into the channel.

Returning to Stone House, I put my catch in a pan of salt water to soak overnight. I would freeze them tomorrow. Soaking them in salt water seemed to make the flesh of the fish taste better. Everyone has their opinion, and that is mine. I made some supper and ate it. I then sat down in my recliner to watch some news. At around eleven, my phone wakened me from my slumbers. I didn't see much of the news. I answered the phone to find it was Javier.

"Hello," I said, "this is Pastor Jack speaking."

I heard the distinctive voice on the other end of the line reply, "Hello, Jack, do you know who this is?"

I responded, "Javier, how nice to hear your voice!"

"Do you really mean that, or are you just being nice?" he asked. Answering his own question he continued, "I guess you mean it, because you don't put on for anyone as far as I can see. You're a pretty much a what-you-see-is-what-you-get person up to a point."

I said, chuckling, "I think you just paid me a compliment, of sorts."

I could hear a smile in his voice. "Indeed, against my better judgment, I really like you. It makes my job much more difficult to do, though."

I replied, "I can imagine. To what do I owe the honor of this call?"

His reply was in no way surprising. "There are people here who really are displeased with your choice of a senior pastor. They are accusing our office of failing in our efforts to control the situation."

I burst in. "Are they under the impression that I work for them or something?" I asked incredulously.

He replied, "No, they just are not accustomed to working with people who are not easily manipulated. You don't respond to the usual methods of manipulation. In fact, you have been ahead of us at every point along the way as was your friend, Dr. Lucas. It is hard for our people here to handle defeat."

I pondered that for a couple of minutes and then said to him, "Javier, I am not your enemy nor am I their enemy!"

His reply was both surprising and sobering. "I know that, but you need to know that they are your enemy. They will try to destroy you if they can't manipulate you. That's what they do."

"My friend," I said, "I don't know how to respond to that. I have been playing defense since this began because I do not wish to be the aggressor, but what am I to do?"

I heard sympathy in his voice as he responded, "I don't know, Jack. You are in a difficult spot. Your friend did not do you any favors throwing you into this position."

"That's true," I said, "I do not intend, however, to betray his trust nor fail in my work. Doc Lucas's trust in me is something that I hold close to my heart. God being my helper, I will not let him down, if it costs me my life!"

After a brief pause, Javier replied, "It may cost you just exactly that."

That got my hackles up just a bit, and I said in reply, "I think you'll find that taking my life is no easy matter!"

That made him laugh right out loud. "We already know that from hard experience. You have uncanny survival skills. Once could be fluke, but have avoided our traps more times that you even know. My bosses are mystified as to how you do that."

I replied, "Some instincts you never lose, but I have to give most of the credit to God. The first attempt on my life was foiled by a mosquito. I was trying to avoid one outside my house just as your assassin fired. Once I was apprised that I needed to be careful, my training and experience kicked in."

He came back with, "What training and experience? We have not been able to find any indication that you ever had any such training."

"And you never will," I said. "Some things are intended to remain buried. There are secrets that remain so because there is no record to find. The knowledge of them dies with those who were involved."

I could hear frustration in his voice, "Did Dr. Lucas know of your training?"

I replied, "Not to my knowledge. I never told him. In fact, I have never told anyone, not a soul. Doc had instincts about people that were almost supernatural, maybe they were supernatural. I don't know. I do know this. I'd give up all this and more to be able to discuss some of this stuff with him."

Javier said softly, "A wise and trustworthy friend is hard to find. I'm sorry that you lost him."

I let the fact that he had been instrumental in Doc's death pass and said, "Well, new players, new game. You need to tell your people that, because it is the truth that we are dealing with here."

He said, "They are not going to like that. They are accustomed to throwing money or muscle at a problem and solving it. In your case neither one has worked yet. Maybe they aren't throwing enough of either. I wish I could get a sense of what we need to do to resolve this."

"I have an idea," I said. "How about you just leave me alone and let me do my job without hanging over my shoulder and shooting at me!"

He sighed. "I wish we could, but that is not going to happen now. You've made us look too bad; there's too much pride on the line now. They're coming after you. I'll try to give you a warning, but I'm not sure that I'll be able to do that. I think it'll be a few months before they move. They are trying to plan a strategy that will take you down without hurting anyone. Please understand, though, if that doesn't work, they'll want blood. That would be yours."

CHAPTER 26

I sat for a long time after hanging up without moving, not really thinking about anything specific, but was allowing my mind to drift in the general vicinity of the discussion we had just had on the phone. I wished people weren't so protective of their perceived "turf." That just makes things more difficult. The only thing that gave them the right to make demands was their wealth, strength, and pervasive reach. It just didn't seem as though there was anything I could do. It was a classic David and Goliath situation. Without a doubt they would take action when they thought it necessary or appropriate. After all, they had murdered Doc Lucas. There was no doubt they would do the same again whenever they felt they needed to and however seemed to be the most expeditious way for them. They would try to make it look like an accident, and there were many ways to do that. Maybe they needed to be reminded that Goliath had not fared so well the day he met David.

I ran my hands through my hair and came to a decision. I was going to keep on doing my job. I was not going to hide and live in fear. I was going to continue to study Doc Lucas's research and let God shake out the details. I couldn't imagine that the Lord brought me here to have my life taken from me, but it was his to do with what he saw to be the best thing. I have learned to be content doing God's will no matter what that means. There is no point in changing that tack now. I really do believe that God always knows what he is doing and he always has my best interest and his glory in mind. I am perfectly content to live that out. In fact, it has occurred to me that some may think that God is the ultimate egotist, since he always is glorified. If you think about it, though, God is not seeking his glory. He is glory! Since in the New Jerusalem, there will be no need of the sun because the Son will light that world, we might understand that in order for us to know him, we must join in glorifying him, because that is the "job" of heavenly beings. So to live to the glory of God is to begin heaven's work on earth!

With that decided, I headed for bed because it was after midnight. No doubt things would look better in the morning. If not better, they would at least look different. Sometimes a new perspective was as good as a change of scenery. With that thought in mind I dozed off and did not awaken until the early hours of the morning. It was about six when my eyes opened. I started my morning routine with a pot of coffee brewing and a hot shower. Once dressed, I sat down at my desk with a cup of coffee and did some reading. It occurred to me that I should give Doc's notes more attention. Since I had finished the journals that I had out, I opened the hidden safe and put the two back in that I had finished and took the next one out.

After breakfast, I sat down with Doc's next journal and started reading. In this journal, Doc was reporting some research that he had done regarding genetic manipulation. As I read, I was fascinated by what he was postulating. He wrote:

In studying the advances in genetic research/manipulation, it has occurred to me that the mark of the beast may be something like this. One thing that has always puzzled me is that the acceptance of the mark of the beast is irreversible. Once accepted it cannot be undone. According to the Word, all manner of sin will be forgiven men except blasphemy against the Holy Spirit. This did not appear to be that kind of thing. What if the acceptance of the mark of the beast is a genetic alteration that causes the person to become some kind of hybrid humanoid rather than a man/woman as God created us?

I stopped reading there because my head was about to explode. Could it be? Doc apparently thought it was a possible scenario, it didn't seem prudent for me to reject it out of hand, but it seemed so science-fictionesque that it almost made me laugh. As I thought about it, it occurred to me that by accepting a genetic alteration that altered their humanity, people might be excluding themselves from the grace God offers humankind in Christ Jesus. I also wondered what Doc had come across in his research that had sent his mind down that road? I would need to dig deeper, but I had a staff meeting to attend.

The meeting was mostly about the logistics of moving the new senior pastor. There were a number of logistical matters to work on. Some of the members wanted to send a group of men and boys to help the family move. They were trying to save money. After several minutes of discussion, it was decided to hire a professional moving company to take care of the work. They would pick them up, load the truck, and unload it for them when they arrived. It was suggested that we take photos of the house and measurements of the rooms so that they could look it over. That seemed like a really good idea. Jerry Preston, the youth pastor, said his wife had suggested it and wanted to do it. I gave him Pastor Longstreet's e-mail address so they could send the photos. That reminded me, I was going to have to ask him if he was in any way a descendant of General Longstreet. Not that it mattered, it was just something that interested me. The staff meeting ended after about an hour. Although I always tried to remain congenial, I really did not like board meetings, staff meetings, and the like. I felt they were well-named, just incorrectly spelled.

As I was leaving the meeting, James asked if he could have a few minutes, so we went into my office.

"How's it going, James?" I asked him.

"That's what I wanted to talk with you about," he replied. "Sarah will not leave me alone. She is calling me and demanding to meet with me. I have told her over and over that she will have to meet me in my office if she wants to talk, but she won't do it. She keeps insisting that I come to her apartment or she come to mine. I have refused, but wanted you to know about it."

I said to him, "You know what she is trying to do, right? She is trying to get you into a compromising situation and probably would have another friend take some photos of you that could be photoshopped to make you look bad. Thanks for letting me know about this. This kind of openness goes a long way toward establishing trust."

He said, "I just can hardly believe that she would do that, but it appears that you were right about her. She has also stopped coming to church. I guess when she lost what control she had, she walked away."

"That's the way it looks to me," I replied. "I'm encouraged that you came to me with this. Keep me in the loop, okay?" He said he would and left my office.

My stomach told me that it was lunchtime. I looked at my watch, and it did not disagree. I decided to run down to a local restaurant where I had heard they made an excellent Italian sub sandwich. It was only a couple of miles from the church, so I drove quickly down there. While I was waiting for a table, by the way I have found that a line in a restaurant is usually a good sign, I looked up and saw Sarah across the dining room. I waited until I had been seated and ordered, then I walked over to her table. She acted surprised to see me. "Oh, Pastor!" she exclaimed. "I didn't see you over there," she said with a smile.

"Over where?" I replied. She looked flustered, and I said. "Don't pretend you didn't see me come in. You are better trained than that." Her eyes became very cold as she stared at me. "Look," I said, "James has been reporting to me about your efforts to compromise him. He is not going to fall for it, so you might as well give up and move on. We're closing ranks, and you will not be able to penetrate or compromise us."

She gave me a most hateful look and replied angrily, "You have no idea what or who you are messing with here! The will kill you, and I hope they do!"

I smiled at her, not sure where that came from, and replied, "They have already tried several times, and I've no doubt they'll try again. I don't know exactly what is so important that a church will kill for it, but I am figuring it out. I have some answers, but not all of them. I think that I will eventually put it together. Until then, you might just as well stop bothering James. He isn't interested."

She angrily spat out, "What are you? His guardian angel?"

"Something like that." I chuckled. And I went back to my table. I did notice that she left immediately without finishing her lunch. I guess I was bad for her digestion.

CHAPTER 27

I was seated at my desk reviewing the changes in my life. Sunday we would celebrate the completion of my first year as executive pastor of Stone Church. It had been an eventful year. Since the passing of my old friend, Doc Lucas, there had been a number of "events" that occurred. I had been shot at, attacked by thugs, burglarized, and threatened. All of these, I had survived. The protection of the Almighty had both defended me and guided my steps. As I gave thanks, I thought about Javier and wondered how he was doing. I did not have any way of getting in touch with him. I hoped that he was well.

There has also been some major staff changes with the sudden death of the senior pastor and his replacement. That did not even take into account the conflicts fomented by Sarah Harris, if that were really her name, between myself and some of the staff members. It seemed like that had been controlled. Over all, it had been a good year. Attendance was up, and the staff was doing a wonderful job of ministering in the local community. We were planning our first Bible conference to be hosted at our church. The date was still about six months away. Most of the staff was excited about it. Some just saw it as additional work. They were right about that.

It was still early in the day, so I decided to go to the boathouse and the office above it. There were a bunch of journals there that I had not looked at. It was high time that I started looking at them. I drove down to the locked gate above the boathouse and walked down the path, climbed down the ladder, and entered the boathouse using the entrance code. As I entered the office, I checked out all of the cameras. There didn't seem to be anything going on that was noteworthy.

I opened the first of the file cabinets and took out one of the journals. I started reading Doc's notes. He had written:

> It is clear that the technology available today would enable a small group of people to exert domination over the people of the earth. There is technology in development that would enable a dictatorial power to implant a programmable microchip into the human body that would accept uploads. These could also be used in conjunction with genetic manipulations. With these changes controlled by the chip, the government would be able to control the population by genetic/emotional/mental manipulation. It appears to be a counterfeit version of the new birth. At the moment of the new birth, God implants the "seed of Christ" in our hearts. As we grow in grace, we become more and more like Christ until the moment when we are changed into his likeness.

The antichrist is going to use genetic/cyber implants to try to achieve the same effect in his minions.

These implants will probably change the people who accept them into subhuman, superhuman, or humanoid beings who are no longer under the covenant of grace. By accepting this manipulation, they will be swearing allegiance to the beast. This will very likely be used also as a solution to overpopulation, much as Adolf Hitler used the extermination of undesirables in Europe during WWII. Rather than exterminating them, however, they will just be allowed to starve to death in the kingdom of antichrist.

I sat thinking over what I had just read. It reminded me of an article that I had read about some of the medical implants that had been used in Europe that had so integrated themselves into the subjects' bodies that there had been danger in removing them for fear that the endocrine system had become dependent on the electronic stimulus and would not resume their natural functions. The specific fear was that the subjects' brains had become lazy and would not resume the work that the implant had been doing.

Also, it occurred to me that if the implant were programmable and it could be used to stimulate various parts of the brain, the brain activity could be almost completely taken over by "outside" forces. Through the scanners in banks, schools, hospitals, government buildings, etc., updates to the programs that controlled people could be downloaded uniformly and collectively. It was a really insidious plan. The worst part of it is that it is simple and it just could work.

Returning to Doc's journal I read this:

> The scale of this research and plan would require billions of dollars to sustain it. What is the source of the funding? I know that the Catholic Church is involved. They have the shroud of Turin, but somebody is bankrolling this. Finding the source of the money and we will have a closer understanding of the motivation behind the project.

I closed and locked up the journal and returned to my car. It occurred to me that somebody may have seen me come here without taking the boat out, so I took the pontoon boat out onto the river for a short ride. I didn't fish because fishing requires too much concentration and I wanted to think. It occurred to me that I would need to know that name of the project before I could trace the funding. It was a major assumption that I could trace the funding anyway. Then another thought struck my mind, the one place where funding could flow without much suspicion or notice being taken was the United Nations. The Vatican had an ambassador to the United Nations as did most other nations of the world. Much of the leg work for such a project could be carried out under the umbrella of the UN without raising much, if any, attention. How would one ever chase down the loose ends of such a project?

Cruising back up the channel, I put the pontoon back in the boathouse and headed back up to my car. When I got to my car, the driver's side window was broken. I called the police and waited for them to arrive. They asked if I had any idea who might do that. I told them no. I also told them that, as far as I could see, there was nothing missing. When they were finished checking it over, I drove home and called my insurance agent. They told me to take it to a local auto glass shop and they would fix it.

It had been a busy day, and I was tired and hungry. After a light dinner, I sat down to watch some news on TV. At around eleven, I went to bed.

The next morning, I called the auto glass shop and they told me that they could do it right away if I would bring it up, so I did. The proprietor was a very friendly man from Mexico. It really made me happy because it gave me an opportunity to practice speaking Spanish a little bit. He told me about his family. He said he had a daughter who worked for the United Nations, which piqued my interest. I asked him if she worked in New York City, and he told me no, she worked in Mexico City. When I asked him what she did in Mexico City, he said that she was the coordinator for several United Nations orphanages in Mexico that they ran in conjunction with the Catholic Church. Now, I was really listening. I asked him if one the orphanages was near a place called San Rafael. He said that he knew of that one, because it was near where he lived before moving to the USA. He did not know about any of the others, but it was enough to "unofficially confirm" that what Doc had thought was at least possible, maybe even probable.

The technician came out and advised me that my car was finished, so I left. Fortunately, the cost was covered by my insurance, so there was no out of pocket. I said adios to my new friend and headed down the road. I did take the time to explain that I was a pastor and invited him to Stone Church.

As I was driving away from the glass shop, I noticed that there were sticky spots on the back of the steering wheel. I ran my fingers lightly around it and found several spots around an inch wide that were sticky. I decided to stop by the police station and add that piece of information to the police report. The officer to whom I reported the information mentioned that it sounded like somebody had been trying to lift fingerprints off the steering wheel. That information caused me to consider thoughtfully the question of, "Why would anybody want my fingerprints?" It also caused me some amusement, because they probably did not realize that I was not the only one that drove that Caddy.

CHAPTER 28

About two weeks after the incident where the window of my car was broken, I received quite a surprise. I was seated at my desk when Jennifer buzzed me on the phone. She said that I had a visitor. I knew that I had no appointments set for today, so I asked her who it was. She replied that it was a man named Javier and he spoke with an accent. I immediately told her to escort him in, which she immediately did.

I greeted Javier with genuine pleasure. "My friend, how are you? It is good to see you. This is an unexpected pleasure."

He replied, "It is good to see you as well. This is not, however, a social call."

"Well," I responded, "whatever the reason, I'll take pleasure in your visit."

"Do you always put the best construction on every situation?" he questioned.

"The truth is, no," I replied. "But I do try my best to do that. Life is too short to spend it looking for an ulterior motive behind every action. If there is one, it usually manifests itself soon enough."

At that he smiled. "Always ready with your wit and wisdom, aren't you?" he said. "Look, let me get to the reason for my visit. My bosses don't know that I'm here, although they will probably find out eventually."

I replied, "They won't hear it from me."

He said, "They won't need to. They have your place under surveillance. They know who comes and goes from here. I wore a disguise, but they will probably figure it out eventually."

That puzzled me. "Why did you take the chance?" I asked.

"Because I have come to regard you as a friend. I know that I should not allow myself to feel that way, but it is what it is. You have been so straightforward with me and us. There doesn't seem to be any deception in you. You are very cunning and adept at this game, but you are not a liar or a sneak. It is a combination that intrigues me. I really like you and don't want to see you hurt. You have to know that you are playing a very dangerous game and could get yourself killed in the process."

I reached over and took Javier's hand. "Thank you, my friend. I thank you for your concern. Whatever happens to me is somewhat immaterial. Please know that I will not hold you responsible. My life is in God's hands, as was Doc's. I wish you could have known him better."

He dropped his head and replied, "I do too. You know, I don't think that I have ever so misread a situation as I have this one. Doc was much more clever than we gave him credit for, and his *coup de gras* was picking you to follow him. You have been ahead of us at every turn."

I held up my hand and said, "It isn't me. There has been a divine guidance with me from the beginning of this ministry. Don't give the credit to me. It is the work of God. Give him the credit for what he does."

"So you don't think it's your spy craft that has kept you alive?" he asked.

I replied, "Not hardly, when you're working in the Lord's vineyard, you must learn to rely on his protection. My primary work is not trying to figure out what you are doing, it's the propagation of the gospel through the local church. Following up on Doc's research is just something that I do in my spare time. As far as what your bosses want to do to or with me, I don't worry much about it. Until I have fulfilled what God has for me to do here, they will be ineffective. When he is finished with me, it will no longer matter."

Javier gave me a long look and said, "That's a rather fatalistic view, isn't it?"

"Not really," I replied. "I'd say it's more realistic. You see, your people just think they are calling the shots. I believe what Jesus said when he was before the Roman judge, which was basically, 'You can do nothing unless my Father in heaven allows it.' That is my view. They are powerless unless it is God's time and way. What do I have to fear from his will? It's not that I am fearless, I just fear God more than I fear them."

He regarded me for a long moment and said, "I'm going to regret losing you. I would really enjoy hours of deep conversation with you. We could have great discussions. Although my faith is not like yours, I would aspire to trust God as you do. It is so simple and uplifting. As complex as your life is, your faith is so basic and simple."

I replied, "Think of it as a compass. The principle is pretty simple. From true north, you can find your way anywhere, but you must first find true north. I trust God to point me to true north and from there, I can find my next step. You know, the Word says that God is light. The psalmist says, 'Thy word is a lamp to my feet and a light to my pathway.' We sometimes assume that means that we can see the way ahead, but it might mean that we can merely see the next step. If we really trust God, we can take that step with confidence whether we can see beyond it or not."

"You make me want to know and trust God as you do," Javier said. "It seems like you trust God as you would a friend."

"That is exactly how it is," I replied. "To know him is to trust him."

Javier studied me for a few moments of silence then said, "I was hoping to convince you to abandon this quest for your own safety and find myself thinking that it would be more dangerous for you to do that than continue. You seem to be impervious to our attacks as long as you are doing what the Lord has given you to do. I just want you to be careful. Our people are going to come after you in ways that they have not done, so far."

I smiled at him and replied, "I am expecting that. I even have some ideas of how they might attack. I would like to warn you of something, if I may. I believe that your leaders are literally making a deal with the devil in order to work this project. You need to be careful yourself. Whoever is financing this project is going to want to control it. They have stayed in the background during the development of the cloning process, but they are planning to take control of the whole thing. They will turn on you when they have what they want. Please watch your back, my friend. You could be very vulnerable."

He looked stunned and said, "How much do you know?"

I replied, "What I have is things that I have surmised from a few facts. I am aware that you are in the process of cloning the body of Jesus from the blood on the shroud of Turin. In fact, that project is quite advanced. I overheard a couple of people talking in Mexico and put together that many of the people working in the project think that they are facilitating the second coming of Christ. What they don't know is that the people behind the financing do not have such pure motives. They plan to use the clone for a power grab. They are working on DNA splicing that will make people who swear allegiance to them genetically altered followers of this false Christ. In fact, it is my suspicion that he will be the beast spoken of in Daniel and Revelation. Once you and your friends have served your purpose, you will be eliminated. Thus the secrecy of the project is mandatory. That is why they want you to eliminate me."

Javier looked at me in shock. "You have figured out more than I have. I never thought about the price we might have to pay for the generous donation that backed this project. It's similar to Herod telling the wise men to let him know once they found the king so that he too could go and worship. I'm not sure what the source of the funding is. I never thought to ask. Asking now might just get me kicked off the project or worse."

I responded, "I'm pretty sure that this funding was facilitated around the United Nations. There is a lot of unaccounted funding that flows around at that place."

"You may be right about that," he conceded. "Now you're making me sound like a conspiracy theorist!" he exclaimed.

"You would do well to watch your back," I said. "You just don't know who you can trust anymore."

He said ruefully, "Well, at least I know why they are so upset with what you are doing. You have uncovered more than any other one person."

"Don't forget Doc," I said. "He was the one that figured it out. I'm just tying together the loose ends that he left."

Javier nodded. "He was truly a remarkable man. What got this whole investigation started anyway?"

"Well," I replied, "we were talking a few years back during one of our many sessions where any idea was worth flinging out to take a look at. We had been talking about the end times and the deceptive mastery of the antichrist, and I might have mentioned that the ultimate deception would be for the antichrist to be walking around in the cloned body of Jesus. We didn't discuss it further, and I thought that must have sounded ridiculous to Doc and forgot about it. I didn't think he took it seriously until I started reading the results of some of the research that he had done subsequently. So I suppose you could say I stumbled into the truth like a blind pig finding a truffle."

After a studied look from Javier, he said, "That could only be divine revelation coming to you. It's too off the wall for anything else."

I chuckled. "I admit that after saying it out loud, it felt like it was off the wall, like tracking UFOs."

"And yet it was not," he replied softly.

Javier stood to his feet. "I must go," he said. "We may never meet again on this earth. I think that we will not. Maybe somewhere, sometime in eternity we will be able to really share our hearts as friends."

"I would very much like that, Javier. Good friends are hard to find and should be held dearly," I replied.

"*Vaya con, Dios.*" He gripped my hand, and without another word, he walked out of my office and probably out of my life. I felt sad.

CHAPTER 29

After the anniversary service, life settled into a comfortable routine. I did a little travelling to attend a couple of Bible conferences. We held our Bible conference, which was well-attended. It occurred to me that we should have a special Fourth of July celebration. I thought it would be nice to have a hog roast on the church grounds. In fact, I decided to have an open house at Stone House and open it up to guests for the day. The offices and sleeping quarters could be locked so that people could roam the place and enjoy a good time. We appointed a committee from the church to handle the plans.

On the day of the event, there were literally hundreds of people who came and went from the property. I did not recognize all of them, but we did invite the community as well as the church regulars. I saw Sarah Harris mingling with the crowd. I made it a point to meet and greet her. She was pleasant enough, but not very friendly. I moved on through the guests, trying to make sure everyone was having a good time.

As I was chatting with people, I saw an old friend of mine from college days. His name was Mike Mason, and I had not seen him for years. His nickname was M&M when we were young. It turns out that he was teaching at a university in a neighboring state. We met and shook hands. "Mikey!" I exclaimed, giving him a big hug. "It has literally been years since I've seen you. You look about the same, just more mature-looking."

He laughed. "That must be the new, gentle way of telling people they are getting old. You look good, but more mature as well."

"Well, I hope I am," I replied. "What brings you here?"

He answered, "I have a cousin in your church, and she invited me to come and spend the day. I needed a break, so I headed over."

"I'm really glad you came. By the way, do you have a place to stay?" I asked.

"Well, I was just going to check into one of the local hotels," he said.

"No, you're not going to do that. You will stay here, with me," I said.

He asked, "Are you sure about that?"

I replied, "Absolutely. I have this big old house and very little company. There are five guest rooms, so take your pick. Did your wife come with you?"

"Yes, she did. She's over there visiting with my cousin."

I said, "Unpack your stuff at your leisure and stay as long as you like."

He replied, "I really appreciate this. I hope it's not an inconvenience."

"No way!" I said. "It's my pleasure. I can't wait to catch up a bit, once things slow down a little here."

As the party was winding down, I saw Sarah Harris talking with a rather large man. Their conversation seemed somewhat heated, or at least animated. The heated part may have been my interpretation, but it was decidedly a lively conversation. I was walking past when she broke away from him and asked if she could speak with me. I told her, "Of course. What's on your mind?"

She asked, "Can't we go somewhere more private?"

At that, I instantly felt my hackles rise. I guided her over to a bench that was on the grounds but out in the open and invited her to sit down. She gave me a disgusted look and sat down, so I sat down beside her with a safe gap between us.

When we first sat down, she started making small talk. After a few minutes I said to her, "Sarah, I don't mean to be insensitive, but this is a really busy day for me. What is it that you wanted to talk about?"

She kept glancing over her shoulder. I resisted the temptation to see who she was looking at. Instead, I looked around for something that would show me via a reflection. There was a big sliding glass door on the back of the house that gave me a pretty good angle. The guy that Sarah had been talking with just before asking me if we could talk had maneuvered his way behind us and was making a video with his phone. He gave her a nod, and she suddenly started acting angry. She pushed me back and started screaming at me. She said, "You can't just break it off with me like that! After all the nights together and all the times we've had! You said we would get married!" Then she threw her arms around me. I extricated myself from her embrace and got up.

Walking quickly to the man who was making the video, I confiscated his phone and threw it into the goldfish pond in the backyard. He was aghast and started sputtering at me. I held up one finger and looked him in the eye. I said, "If I were you, I would not make this any worse than it is. You tried to set me up, and it didn't work. You should leave while you are even. Anything that happens from here will be a losing proposition for you." He started toward the pond to retrieve his phone. "Stop right there!" I told him. "Just leave it in the pond." I turned to Sarah and said, "Unless you are attending a church service, to which everyone is welcome, you are not welcome on this property anymore. Go with your friend." They left in a hurry, both casting ugly looks over their shoulders at me.

My friend Mike asked me, "What is going on here?"

I replied, "Probably just some kind of prank that they can put online. You know, something like, 'Look what we caught the preacher doing!'"

He looked puzzled. "Why would they do that?" he asked.

"Some people will do anything for a sensational upload. They don't care whether it's true or not. Sarah used to come to church here, but it's been a good while since she has been here. Maybe she's bitter about something. It could have been something I said."

Mike laughed at that. "I guess we all could be accused of stepping on a few toes from time to time. You can't preach the Word of God for very long without stepping on toes."

"That's a fact," I replied.

"Aren't you worried about people talking?" he asked.

"Worried? No," I replied. "It is inevitable that people will talk. I'd rather they talk about what I did to him than what she said to me. That's easier to deal with."

"You are probably right about that. Actually, that was quite brilliant. Most people would never think of that," he said.

"Well, blame it on God. It was not a considered response. It just happened like it happened. Except, I really don't believe that things happen like that. God just diffused a potentially devastating situation by creating a more sensational one. I see his wisdom in that, but can't take credit myself," I responded. "Come on, let me show you to your suite."

CHAPTER 30

It was disgusting that I let Sarah Harris and her henchman maneuver me into a potentially compromising spot. I did remember to go out and fish his phone out of my fishpond. It was one of those fancy waterproof cell phones. No wonder he tried to rescue it. I erased his video and then opened the phone up and removed the SIM card. I crushed the card under my heel and then threw it in the still hot grill directly onto the red hot coals. "Good luck retrieving anything from that," I thought.

Mike and Annie, his wife, came down to the den after unpacking and freshening up a bit. "Are you hungry?" I asked them.

"Not right now," they both said. I was not surprised.

"Would you like to go out and watch some fireworks? The city has a great display. If you don't want to go out, we could watch the national fireworks display on TV. That's always good. What is your pleasure?

They looked at each other with questioning looks. Annie said, "I would prefer a live fireworks display, if it is not too inconvenient."

Mike said, "That would be great, if we can swing it."

"It is as easy as jumping into the car and driving about three miles. They do the fireworks over the river at ten o'clock. We should leave about eight thirty, or we won't get a decent spot from which to watch. We'll plan on it," I replied.

We drove to the fireworks arriving around nine o'clock. The crowds were already getting thick in Riverside Park. We brought along some lawn chairs, and Mike's cousin and her family joined us. So we had a noisy group of eight people. It was a good time, and the fireworks were spectacular. They had music from a local radio station that was synchronized with the fireworks. They started with "Stars and Stripes Forever" and ended with "The 1812 Overture," so life was good. I invited Mike's cousin and her family back to the house to visit and have some leftovers from the afternoon. There was more pulled pork left over than I would eat in a lifetime. So they came.

Arriving back at the house at around eleven, we ate pork, potato salad, along with cake, cookies, and all manner of goodies. They finally left a little past one in the morning. I was tired but wound up like an eight-day clock.

Annie went to bed, and Mike and I sat down and chatted for another half hour to forty-five minutes. He started yawning and headed off to bed. I set the alarm at exactly 1:58 p.m. I'm not sure why I remember, but I do. I hit the sack and was out like a light.

I was dreaming that I was helping my grandfather build my aunt's house that we built after my uncle was killed. The hammers were banging and banging. Finally my conscious mind crawled out of the fog, and I realized that somebody was banging on the door. I put on a pair of sweat pants and a robe and went to the door. It was the police, and they did not come bearing good news.

"Good morning, officers," I said. "What brings you to my door so early in the morning?"

A man in street clothes said, "Good morning, sir. I am Detective Art Jackson. Are you Jack Spencer?"

"Yes, I am," I replied. "Why do you ask?"

"Do you know Sarah Harris?" he asked.

"I do know her, but I'm a bit curious as to why that would bring you to my door," I replied.

"When is the last time you saw her?" asked Detective Jackson.

"Yesterday afternoon when she left the hog roast, which I believe was around 6:00 p.m., was the last time I saw her. Although I did not check the time, I think it's a fairly accurate estimate," I replied. "What is this all about, anyway?"

"We'll ask the questions, if you please," replied the detective. I started feeling distinctly uncomfortable with that response.

"You may ask your questions, but I think I have a right to know what is going on. If you expect me to be forthright with you, you might try being upfront with me," I replied. "I don't know what happened, but for your information I have an alibi for every moment since she left until this very one. So what happened?"

"Sarah was found dead at around midnight last night. She was strangled and your fingerprints were found there, so I'm not sure about your alibi. It had better be good," said Detective Jackson.

I told him, "I had house guests last evening who were with me until I went to bed at around 2:00 a.m. We went to the fireworks down at the park and then came home and visited until the wee hours. There were six or seven people in our party and a number of other acquaintances that saw me at the fireworks with them. We arrived home after the fireworks and were here together for the rest of the evening. They can verify that from the time of the hog roast until I went to bed I was with them. When I went to bed, I set the burglar alarm, which will verify that no doors or windows were open during the night. We also have surveillance cameras on the property. You will be able to verify that I did not leave the property alone during the evening and night. Do you have any other questions, Detective?"

"You can prove that?" he asked.

"Indisputably!" I replied.

"We had heard that you and Ms. Harris had some kind of disagreement yesterday afternoon. It was suggested that you might have had a reason to shut her up," the detective said.

"We had no disagreement. She tried to imply that we had some kind of relationship, which we never had. There was a friend of hers trying to tape the incident on his phone."

"What was her friend's name?" asked Detective Jackson.

"I didn't know him, and he did not introduce himself to me. He was a pretty average-looking guy, though. He was around 5'10" and probably would have weighed around 175. He had light brown hair and blue eyes. I don't remember any scars or distinguishing marks on him," I told him.

"That's a pretty good description of the guy that told us that you had a disagreement with Sarah," he said. "He said that you spoke quite angrily to her."

"Detective, I can give you the names of twenty or more people who were there during the time that didn't even know anything happened. That's how heated the discussion became. We were right out in the open on a bench beside the fishpond. If we had a knockdown drag out, everyone there would have noticed. Why don't you show up here tomorrow after church and you can interview anyone that is willing to talk to you?" I offered.

"We'll check out your alibi and get back with you. If it's as ironclad as you say, we'll have to take another tack on the investigation. It seemed like a slam dunk, when we arrived here this morning," the detective said.

"If you want, some of the people are still here. I would have to wake them, but I will do so, if you want to wait a few minutes," I said. I seated the detective in the living room and gave him coffee and then went up to awaken Mike and Annie. They were quite groggy, but when I explained the situation, all sleep left their eyes and they were ready to go. I asked them to come down to the living room as soon as they felt comfortable doing so. I went back down to give them time to prepare themselves.

While we were waiting for Mike and Annie, I asked the detective, "Were there any other fingerprints found at the scene?"

He looked at me with some surprise. "Well, yes, but we haven't found a match for them yet. How would you know that?"

I told him about my car being vandalized a few weeks back, explaining how strange it seemed that nothing was taken. Then I told him about finding the sticky spots on the steering wheel. He asked if all this was in the police report. I advised him that I had called the PD and filed an amended report when I discovered the sticky patches because it seemed like someone had lifted fingerprints. What the vandals could not know is that I was not the only one that used that particular car. I told him so and that there was a spare set of keys in the garage so that staff could use the car during the day, if they needed to. I told him they should check to see if any of the prints were Doc's, since he probably didn't ever wipe the car to rid it of his prints. He asked me if I thought my staff would agree to be fingerprinted. I told him that they had to be in order to pass the security check needed to work here. He said that he would check that database.

Just as we were finishing our conversation, Mike and Annie walked into the room. I stepped into my office so that the detective could talk with them without interruption. After he spoke with them for a few minutes, he came into my office and said, "They confirm your story right down to the smallest detail. I came here today to arrest you. Now I don't know what to do."

"Can't help you there," I replied. "Did you get the contact information of the guy that implicated me?"

"Yes, of course," he said. "We document every tip and person of interest, witness, or just a bystander, so we have his contact info."

"He was probably the last person to see her alive. I know that they left Stone Church grounds together. He didn't seem any too pleased either," I told him.

"Why would he be upset?" Detective Jackson asked.

"Well, it seems that he lost his phone. I found it later in the pond. I didn't call him because I didn't know how to get ahold of him," I stated.

"Do you still have his phone?" asked the detective.

"As a matter of fact I do," I replied. "I had completely forgotten about it until now," I told him. "Let me get it for you." I walked into my office and picked up the phone and carried it back out to the officer. As I handed it to him, I noticed that he didn't wear gloves when he handled it. I didn't say anything at the time, but kept it in mind.

"Thank you," he said. "I doubt we'll get much off this since it was in the water, but we'll check it out. By the way, do you have any idea how his phone got into the water?"

I replied, "I suggest you ask him that question." I left it at that. I was not going down that road without an attorney present, but didn't say that to the detective. I was disappointed in myself that I had acted so impulsively. It wasn't that I was angry, but it probably looked like I was. I did not even like the appearance that I acted in anger, because it appeared a little unstable. It wasn't the case, but that is how it would look. It was my hope that he would not open that can of worms. He probably would rather the incident not be memorialized with the police because it represented a failure in his mission, which he would have a hard time spinning with the details in a police report.

Later that afternoon, Detective Jackson called me to tell me that they had found fingerprints from several other staff members and Doc Lucas at the scene. He asked me if I could shed any light on that. I explained to him that somebody, as I had mentioned earlier that day, had broken into my car to grab fingerprints from the steering wheel and other surfaces in the car. Since my entire staff has that car available for their use during the day, there were probably prints from all of them in there. Plus, Doc had driven it before his death. There had never been a reason to wipe it down, so his prints were probably there too. Whoever broke in to steal and copy my fingerprints thought all of the prints in the car must have been mine and had not checked to see what they had. They had made fingerprint pads of prints from every print they found.

It was both a smart move and a very stupid one. Nothing trips up criminals more than their own arrogance. He agreed, and we ended our conversation.

Since Mike was available, I asked him if he would like to speak in our Sunday morning service tomorrow. He said he would, so I made a couple of calls to rearrange the schedule. Since we were all up, I set about putting together a brunch for us. We were a little late eating, so we could hardly call it breakfast. We chatted over brunch about the incident. They were curious about what happened. I told them what I could and explained that Sarah and her partner, whoever he was, were trying to set me up. I explained that I had taken his phone from him and thrown it into the pond. Although he didn't say anything to me, there was little doubt that he was angry over the phone. It took away from him all of the evidence that he had hoped to put online to make me look bad. I wasn't sorry for him, but felt badly about Sarah Harris. She was just a pawn that was eliminated in an effort to bring me down. Had I not had guests, unexpectedly, it would have been very difficult to explain myself. Then it dawned on me that they knew that I lived alone and after Jennifer left, or in the case of the hog roast, the guests, I would normally have been alone. Sarah's murder was a spin-off setup of the failed original setup. The people who wanted my scalp would clearly stop at nothing to get it. I unconsciously rubbed the top of my head and then inwardly chuckled at myself.

Sunday was a nice day, and Mike preached very well. The people were very appreciative of his message. We had dinner, mostly leftovers from the hog roast. I took some of the pork and transformed it into pulled pork. Baked a few potatoes and threw together a salad and there it was. There were plenty of desserts left from the hog roast as well. After lunch and a short visit, they left for home.

274

CHAPTER 31

After Sarah Harris's funeral, which incidentally was held at the cathedral, life settled into a rhythm. There were a number of calls from the police department regarding her murder, but no charges were filed. It looked like I had lucked out again, but I knew there was no luck in it at all. I knew that once again divine providence had intervened before I even knew there was danger and had protected me from a situation that could have compromised the work of Stone Church.

I really regretted the loss of Sarah Harris, because having her around was a contact with Javier and his offices. I could get messages to him through her. That opportunity no longer afforded itself. In addition, I had borne her no malice and truly regretted her untimely death. The situation did let me know exactly the kind of people with whom we were dealing. She had failed in her assignment, and that was how they paid her off. She was just a piece of their machinery to be used to whatever advantage they thought they could gain. When she was unable to entrap me in front of the camera, they killed her and tried to frame me for the murder. Now that they had failed in that, I was curious what their next move would be. Things quieted down instead of intensifying for a time.

Then I received a call from Detective Jackson. He let me know that they had found the guy that was with Sarah on the day of the hog roast and had arrested him and charged him with murder one. Then I understood why things were quiet. Once more, some of their people were going to prison. They were, without a doubt, scrambling to get their guy as good a deal as possible. By my understanding of the law, if he were to plead guilty, he may get life without parole. If he went to trial for murder one and was convicted, he would be eligible for the death penalty. They had more serious things to worry about than me. That was a pleasant thought. It would not be wise to get careless, so I determined that I would not let my guard down. I settled down to doing my work and minding my business.

Once again, I had some time to further pursue the journals that Doc Lucas had left behind. As I was reading through the next one, I discovered that he had begun to research artificial intelligence. He was quite impressed with the progress researchers had made in developing computers that could learn from their environment. He also studied the amazing progress that had been made in putting a powerful processor into a small chip. According to his journal, he found that scientists had been able to reduce a powerful processor into the size of small capsule. He wrote of experiments where the chips were placed in animals and they were actually able to influence the animals' behavior via signals transmitted to the chip. It seemed that the theory behind the research was that by using microchip implants, armies could be influenced to fight with reduced fear reactions. The impulse sent via satellite could override the subjects' natural fears. The research recorded sheep were made to be aggressive and attack other animal which they would normally fear. It seemed that the use of these implants could change behavior by controlling fear and impulse.

Sitting back in my chair, I pondered the data I had just reviewed. I was not an expert on artificial intelligence, but was aware of two things about it. First of all, it was an astounding concept that machines could be programed to learn from and adapt to their environments. Secondly, I knew that this was a rapidly changing field of study.

As I was relaxing and thinking, my phone rang. I answered it to find Steve Lucas speaking to me in very hushed tones. "Jack," he said, "we need to talk."

"Well," I responded, "that is what we are doing."

"No, we need to meet and speak personally, in private."

"Okay," I replied. "Just tell me when and where."

He answered, "How about tomorrow afternoon at the cathedral down the hill from Stone Church?"

"That's fine with me, but seems a bit strange to meet there," I replied.

He said, "I'll explain tomorrow. Can we meet at around 4:00 p.m.?"

"I'll be there," I replied. "See you then."

With that, he hung up and I was left with several large question marks swimming around in my head. I read for a while longer, but nothing popped for me, so I went for a walk. When I came back, I worked in my office in the church for a couple of hours doing paperwork for Stone Church and then went home.

At four o'clock the next afternoon, I walked into the cathedral, but didn't see Steve Lucas anywhere. A little boy walked up to me and handed me an envelope saying a man had given him a dollar to give it to me. I opened the envelope, and there was a sheet of paper. On the paper were these instructions: "Go to the confessional and wait for me." I grinned at the irony of me going to confession and walked down to the booth. I opened the door, entered, and sat down.

A soft voice asked, "Is that you, Jack?" I responded in the affirmative. "It's me, Steve,"

I replied softly, "Hello, Steve. To what do I owe this meeting?"

There was a pause, and then he said, "There have been some changes, and I felt you should know what is going on. Well, the truth is that Javier asked me to talk with you, if I could do so without raising any red flags."

I was surprised and replied, "Okay, why didn't he contact me himself?"

Steve's answer was sobering. "He has been replaced and taken off the project. The powers that be don't trust him to further their plans. He seems to be very taken with you and thinks you are a good person. Frankly, he doesn't think that you deserve what they have planned for you."

I quickly asked, "And what is it that they have planned for me, Steve?"

He said, "They haven't shared that with me as I am not part of the project, but I'm pretty sure that it won't be good. They didn't tell him either, but their typical way of dealing with problems is to eliminate them. They are down to about one option with you. At least that's the way they see it."

I replied, "I don't suppose you have any timetable, do you?"

He said, "No, but it will probably be soon. They are very frustrated with you. Javier said that they have tried to kill you, compromise you, and intimidate you, and nothing seems to work. My dad surely did know his man. You are more like him than any of his own sons. My hat's off to you."

"Thanks," I said, "Doc Lucas was a fascinating man. I guess that I came to know him as most sons can't because we had a meeting of the minds. Our friendship was based more on a parallel than a vertical basis. It makes a difference. He said several times that his sons did not share his passion for truth. I once asked him if he had ever invited any of you into his confidence. He said that he had not, and I thought I detected a sad note in his voice. It's a frightening thing to allow someone else to see us in a vulnerable state. Many times children don't see their parents in that position until they are sick and/or dying."

Again there was silence, then Steve said, "What you just said is going to help me understand the gulf that was between my father and myself once I have digested it. I called to warn you that something is going to happen soon. Be on your guard. I think they are either going to try to kill you or take you. Of the two, killing would be more merciful."

I said softly, "Steve, what you have done tonight is both courageous and dangerous. This could get you killed, and I know that they already tried once. I will not forget this call or the risk you have taken. Do you happen to know who is now in charge of taking care of me?"

He said, "No, I don't. I have some ideas but nothing for sure, but I think you can expect a visit and it won't be friendly. You be careful. You'd better make out your will."

"Wow, that sounds ominous," I replied. "But I will take that under advisement. You take care of yourself. Your dad would be proud of you."

I heard a sharp intake of breath and heard a choked "Thanks. Bye," and he was gone.

I gave him a few minutes and then left the confessional. As a precaution, I left by a different door than the one that I entered. I saw nobody, but did not feel comfortable. It was quite impressive that Steve would risk his life to warn me. I stopped for a cup of coffee on the way home. That gave me time to think in a different atmosphere than my office or home. Sometimes a change of scenery was helpful. Today was not one of those times.

My newly acquired suspicious nature wondered if someone had put him up to make the call to see what I would do. It didn't really matter. Steve's advice about the will was a good idea. My other properties were already under my old will, but the new properties had not been added. I sent an e-mail to Bill Wagner with my will and asked him to add the Stone Church and House properties and to bequeath them to the board of Stone Church upon my demise. I added that I was in no hurry, but one should be prepared. I did not think that anyone could see the calls, texts, and e-mail that I sent from my phone. It was supposed to be secure. I guess I would find out.

When I arrived in my office, it was six in the evening. Jennifer was gone, but there were some messages. I returned a few calls. Most of the people were gone, so I left them messages. That seemed like it was the perpetual cycle of my life. If it was of sufficient importance, a message would eventually result in two people actually having a conversation. If not, it died somewhere on the merry-go-round and was lost to the world to the relief of a few and the knowledge of that same few. Nobody else cared. I chuckled at myself. I was becoming a cynic. Bully for me!

CHAPTER 32

The next morning was a bright Friday, and I decided to take a long drive in the country. Before leaving, I checked my inbox, as Jennifer had been in her office a couple of hours before I arrived in mine. There were a couple of letters to sign and a couple of calls to return. I did that and then headed out after advising Jennifer that I would be out until at least noon.

Out on the road, the countryside was beautiful and the air was fresh. I wasn't going anywhere, but was pretty sure that I would know when I got there. It was about eleven in the morning, and I realized that I had not eaten any breakfast. About ten minutes later, I drove into a very small town with a service station, a small store, a post office, and a small, rather rundown, diner. I pulled into the diner and went inside. It was very country in its décor. There were antiques adorning the place. I looked around seeing a lunch counter around twelve feet long and three tables. There was a middle-aged couple at one of the tables. I sat down at the lunch counter and picked up a menu. A lady came from the kitchen carrying a couple of plates to the couple at the table. When she saw me, her face lit up with a big smile. She chirped out, "Howdy, mister!"

I couldn't help but grin at her. "Howdy, yourself," I responded with about equal enthusiasm.

"Be right with you," she said. I assured her that would be fine and started looking at the menu. I had about decided on the bean soup and a ham sandwich when the waitress walked over with a glass of water and her big smile. "We have some lentil soup that is not on the menu. Folks say it is really good. I also have some fresh cornbread. Does that appeal to you in any way?"

"Ma'am," I replied, "that appeals to me in almost every way. Bring it on! Add a glass of iced tea and I'll be a happy man."

When she brought out the bowl of lentils, I thought she brought out all that she had. The bowl looked to be about the size of a mixing bowl. There was also a stack of about four big pieces of cornbread on the side. She asked me if I like hot peppers with my food. I replied in the affirmative, and she brought out a plate of sautéed serrano chiles. That was about as good a meal as I have ever eaten. I could not believe that I polished off that entire bowl of lentils and three of the pieces of cornbread. She then asked me if I wanted a piece of pie. I declined. I felt like I would burst. As I was settling up the check, she brought out a piece of blackberry pie in a box. "You'll be wanting this later, so I wrapped it up for you. It's on the house. By the way, I noticed that you prayed before you ate. You must be a Christian?"

"Yes, I am," I replied. "I'm pastor of the Stone Church in Fairmont."

Her reply was one of surprise. "Did you know Doc Lucas?" she asked.

"I most certainly did," I replied. "He was one of the best friends I ever had."

"I have to ask your name," she said. "Is it Jack Spencer?"

Now I was the one surprised. "Yes, it is," I replied, "but how could you know that?"

"Well, Doc used to come here several times a year. He would go up to the lake to fish and come down here to eat. He left something here and told me to give it to you, if you ever came along," she said. "I'll go get it for you."

My curiosity was piqued as I waited. She returned with a small metal box, which looked like the boxes that ship specialty cookies and crackers in. She handed it to me with that bright smile. "Come back as often as you can. Any friend of Doc Lucas is in friendly territory here." I thanked her and left the place. I put the metal box on the seat next to me and drove to the lake. I grabbed the box and got out to walk a bit. After that lunch, I needed to move around or I'd fall asleep. I found a comfortable spot on a rock ridge overlooking the lake and sat down. Then I opened the box.

In the box there was a key to a safe deposit box and documents giving me access to the box and its contents. He had also put a map of the lake with the hottest fishing spots. Trust Doc to think of everything. Now I was going to have to make a trip to the bank to see what he had squirreled away there. It occurred to me that Doc had found me to be quite predicable. I was not sure that I liked that idea very well. It looked like I'd be making a trip to the bank in the near future, as soon as I figured out where the bank was located.

Before leaving, I checked at the marina. I knew the answer before I asked the question, but I did not know the details. Doc had a boat at the lake and had prepaid for five years. They put it in the water in the spring and put it in storage for the winter. Doc had already transferred the paperwork in to my name. It was apparent that not even his attorney had known about this getaway. Leave it to Doc.

I drove home and had some dinner. After dinner, I ate that piece of blackberry pie and then looked into the box. The deposit box was at a bank in Clarksburg, a town a few miles to the south. I decided to drive down the next day to see what was in it and what else the old boy had been working on. As the Bible says, "Sufficient unto the day is the evil thereof." In other words, I'd worry about that tomorrow. I had put in a full day and was tired, so I headed for the bedroom after concealing and securing the new key in the floor safe. I thought, "I'm getting paranoid." It caused me a smile remembering that I had recently heard a comedian say, "Just because I'm paranoid doesn't mean that somebody is not out to get me!"

CHAPTER 33

The next morning, I was starting to get ready to go to the bank when it occurred to me that the bank would not be open because it was Saturday. The mystery of the safe deposit box would have to wait until Monday. Since I wasn't scheduled to preach Sunday, I had the day pretty much free. I had breakfast and stepped into my office to see if Jennifer had left anything for me, but there was nothing.

I fired up my computer and started researching further regarding artificial intelligence. The idea of a programmable, implantable device that had the potential to alter a person's perceptions and decision-making processes was both fascinating and frightening. The idea that information could be downloaded onto a device that would interact with the human brain had huge possibilities including the elimination of many mental diseases and learning disabilities. What if educational modules could be downloaded? This may have the potential to replace some school functions. It made for some fascinating speculation, but it appeared that nothing was certain. Nobody was claiming to have successfully downloaded information that the brain was effectively accessing yet. Some thought that it was a matter of time.

I sat back and pondered how such technology would alter human relationships and experiences. Between AI and virtual experience, it appears that we're headed for a synthetic humanity. Even now, Facebook, Twitter, and other social media outlets were synthesizing friendship to shallow sound bites without any social intimacy. The idea of a Facebook friend is antithetical to real friendship. We are living in a world where a witty sound bite is more highly valued than the truth.

What really shook me was the idea that the people controlling the downloads and the content of them could control how people would think. It would be the thought police from the inside out. It is feasible that anyone receiving a download could be "programmed" to think "correctly" regarding religion, politics, economics, and a host of other areas. The idea of belief would become a matter of altering a computer-generated program that could be downloaded to the "chip" and alter the person's thinking. For the first time in history, mind control may actually be within reach of those who might wish to employ it to whatever ends.

I started taking notes furiously, not knowing exactly why I was doing that. Much of the stuff I read about was said to be in experimental stages. It was unclear whether or not they were experimenting on humans yet. No doubt that would come, if it had not already begun. This technology, if it ever was perfected, would be the most lucrative invention in history. The owners could literally control everyone who had an implant.

As I read on, it became clear that the overarching philosophy of those working on AI was humanistic and atheistic. The materials that I was reading came from the point of view that the universe was the center of all and that we serve the universe. If these people would program the downloads, the future of the world looked grim from my point of view.

For the first time in history, I realized, the potential for a small group to truly control the masses was on the horizon. If an elite, ruling class could convince people to accept a programmable chip and it would interact with their brain and nervous system to control their behavior, they could conquer and control human beings. It looked like the mark of the beast was in the development stages. None of the speculative ideas that I had read over the years regarding the mark of the beast made much sense, really. This, however, made lots of sense. It had the flexibility to grow as the field developed.

It was growing dark in my office as I sat there pondering. Suddenly I realized that I was hungry. I had not stopped for lunch or dinner. The day had gone as I had been researching. I looked at my notes and decided that they would be better placed in the safe. I didn't want anyone to come across them and think that I had lost my mind, although I was not so sure myself that I had not.

I drove to a local diner for some dinner. While there, I tried not to think about the stuff I had read throughout the day, but my mind was captive to the idea of AI and its implications. These were just the things that I was aware of, and there were undoubtedly many aspects that were outside my capacity to comprehend just because I was quite ignorant of the field.

CHAPTER 34

Monday morning found me walking into the bank about thirty minutes after it opened. I showed them the papers that Doc had left me and was escorted to the area where the safe deposit boxes were. Once I secured the box, I waited until I was alone and opened it. The first thing that I noticed is that there were two million dollars in bearer bonds. That was a lot of liquidity. In fact, it was more liquidity than I had ever had in my life. There were also around six pounds of gold, which could be quite easily exchanged into cash. There was another letter from Doc. I opened it and read it. It said:

Dear Jack,

In some ways I regret getting you into this situation. I really struggled over who should carry on the work that I had started. Since it was a comment by you that inspired my inquiries into the cloning of Jesus, it seemed right that you be the one. If you are reading this, you have been to the diner up at the lake. There was no doubt in my mind that you would eventually get there.

It occurred to me that you may need to disappear quickly and will need some liquid cash. I am placing around two and a half million dollars in liquid assets in this box. Should you need to go, this will get you a ways down the road. I know that you fly; you will find paperwork and keys to an airplane that is stored in a hanger at the airport up at the lake. Should you need to disappear, take the contents of this box and get away. Don't take foolish chances with your life. That might sound strange coming from me, but life is precious and not to be taken lightly.

I have prayed much for your protection and success. Hopefully, you will be fine. I am quite sure that my life is in danger. If I can see it coming, I may use this windfall myself. If you are reading this, that clearly didn't happen. Be careful and watch your back. You can trust Jennifer. I'm not sure of anyone else.

God bless you, my friend.

Doc

As usual, Doc left more questions than he answered, but it was clear that he understood how dangerous this work was and was prepared to assist me in bailing out, if I chose to do so. The truth was that I wanted to do just exactly that, but was not inclined to go through with it. Nothing that had occurred in my life previously had taught me to back down. It was something that I had never done. I wasn't sure that I knew how. One thing was certain, if Doc was that concerned, I needed to really watch my steps and my back. A partner would really be a blessing about now. The problem is that I would have to trust someone and I wasn't sure who I could trust. This kind of thinking could drive a man crazy.

I put everything back into the box except the airplane papers and key. I thought it might be prudent to give it a test drive, so to speak. It would also be fun. There's nothing like flying over beautiful terrain, and this was certainly that. Looks like I was putting my wings back on.

After a few moments of contemplation, I removed all of the contents of the box and put them in my briefcase. It came to mind that it would be a good idea to have that liquid cash closer at hand than the bank. It was going into the safe at the office. If I needed it, it would be quick. There may not be time to stop by the bank. Besides, once I have visited the bank, it could be watched. Then I chuckled at myself thinking I was becoming paranoid. Steven Lucas's warning was almost constantly on my mind, however.

CHAPTER 35

When I arrived back at Stone Church, there was a car that I didn't recognize parked near the house. I went into the house and through the bedroom to my office. I quickly placed the items from the safe deposit box into the floor safe before checking in with Jennifer. I sat down at my desk and sent her an e-mail, letting her know that I was back. In a few moments, the door opened and she advised me that there was someone there to see me. I asked if I had forgotten an appointment, and she assured me that this was a drop-in. I asked her who it was, and she said it was a priest, but he had not shared his name. I told her to send him in.

When the door opened, it was Javier, my former adversary become friend. I stood and greeted him with a handshake and an embrace. I invited him to sit and said, "Javier, I am delighted and very much surprised to see you here."

He chuckled and replied, "I am pleased that you are happy to see me and do understand your surprise. I'm a bit surprised myself."

I asked him, "What are you doing now? I heard that you were removed from your position."

"Yes," he replied, "I have been ret—I mean I have retired. It was time for me to step down and let the younger men take over."

I was curious. "Did you have any choice in the matter or was it forced on you?"

He looked at me ruefully and said, "I was not nearly ready to retire. I was forced out. They said that I had become ineffective because I lost sight of the mission. They got tired of my trying to get them to leave you alone, I guess."

"I am really sorry about that," I said. "I actually felt that we might be able to work together. Silly me, I guess."

He replied, "That is what they were afraid of. They did not want to work together with Doc Lucas or with you. They just want to stop you, to shut you up."

I was puzzled. "The strange thing, Javier, is that we have never published anything or even talked with anyone else regarding our research. Until we have absolute proof, it would sound too crazy to even talk about it. People would think that we had gone off the deep end."

He replied, "They feel like they can't take the chance on anyone finding out what is happening until they are ready to unveil their plan."

"Javier," I said, "what if their plan gets hijacked? What can or will they do?"

He questioned me, "Who would do that and why?"

"Well," I replied, "for starters, someone with use for such a clone, but a completely different agenda than that of the church."

He scowled at me. "What are you getting at?"

I replied, "Do you know whose money is backing the project? It's possible that funding came because your success would give certain factions a perfect tool for their own use."

He still looked quite perplexed. "I don't get what you are talking about."

"Okay," I replied, "I'll spell it out for you. I would bet, if I were a gambling man, that much of the funding has come from the Middle East. It's possibly from a conglomerate of Muslim influences who have interest in the prophecy of the Twelfth Imam. You have heard of him, have you not?"

"Yes, but I don't see what that has to do with this," he replied.

I continued, "While you think you are bringing about the second coming of Christ, they may be thinking what better way to undermine the kingdom of Christ than by attacking it with a clone of its founder. Not the second coming of Christ, but the advent of the antichrist!"

Now I had his attention. "That's impossible! Preposterous!" he replied.

"Not if you think about it a little," I said. "The Catholic Church has the shroud, which probably contains the best chance of finding viable DNA from Jesus of Nazareth. The only way to get access to it was to partner with the church. You had the shroud and they had access to an almost unlimited amount of cash, which would be needed to make the plan work. They knew they couldn't buy the DNA from you, and they knew that the only real option they had was to wait until the project was complete and steal the finished product. I don't think they anticipated so many would be cloned in order to acquire the perfect clones that they wanted. I suspect that they will make their move very soon now."

Javier looked astounded. He asked me, "How do you come up with these crazy schemes?"

I told him, "Really, it isn't me, Javier, the Bible speaks of the antichrist as one who will come in his own name. He will not acknowledge that Jesus Christ is Lord. His plan is to destroy, if possible, the very kingdom of Christ on earth. It is my opinion that he will be the cloned body of Jesus of Nazareth possessed by the spirit of Satan himself. He is not coming in the name of the Lord. He will, on the contrary, try to wipe the name of Jesus Christ from the earth, most likely with the blood of those who profess faith in him. This looks to me like a perfect opportunity for Satan to secure the vessel that he wants to use to deceive the world."

"How could that be possible?" Javier asked.

"Look at the gospel of *Matthew 24:24, 'For there shall arise false Christs, and false prophets, and shall shew great signs and wonders;*

insomuch that, if it were possible, they shall deceive the very elect.' The only way that the elect could be deceived is for the antichrist to seem so much like Christ that some will believe that he is the promised one rather than Jesus Christ. It is insidious and ugly, but very deceptive, and that is what Satan is good at. He is a liar and the father of lies."

"You may be right," Javier replied, "but what can we do about it?"

I sighed. "Probably not much at this point. Too many people are way too invested in the project to believe anything but what they believe. Not everyone is as honest as you are, Javier."

"Oh!" he exclaimed. "I need to tell you what I came here to tell you. The new boss, the guy that took my place is a retired soldier who came to the church and became a priest. He says that he knows you."

"Really!" I replied. "What is his name?"

"He is known these days as Father McKinnley, but was Sergeant McKinnley in the British Special Forces. He says that he remembers you, but didn't seem to have much affection for you."

"I remember him. Brian McKinnley is his name. He is, or at least was, a very evil man. He had a streak of cruelty that showed up from time to time. The last thing I remember about him was that he raped and killed a young boy. He thought that nobody would find out, but the boy's older brother saw him do it and reported him. He was to be brought up on charges, but he deserted the night before his trial. Until today, I never heard from him or of him again. At the time I too was a different man and wanted to kill him with my bare hands. It would have taken some doing, but I thought that I was up to it. I no longer have that desire. I would leave him to the mercy of a judge and jury and then to the mercies of God. I hope he has found peace with his past."

Javier looked positively aghast as I related my acquaintance with his colleague. "That would explain his lack of affection for you. Your testimony could make him look bad. In fact, it might get him defrocked."

"I doubt that," I replied. "That was a long time ago, and I'm not looking to dig up bones. On another note, I doubt that he would cut me any slack at all, if and when we meet."

Javier said, "That may be sooner than you think. He is coming for you, soon. Please beware. I don't trust him, and he seems to take way too much pleasure in the strong arm side of his work."

"Some things never change," I replied. "What are they going to do with you?"

He shrugged. "If they knew that I had come here, they would kill me for sure. I snuck into town under an assumed name and in disguise. I'll slip out the same way. If this ever blows over, I would very much enjoy rekindling our friendship. What do you think about that?"

I smiled at him and said, "Javier, I would love that. It would be an honor to call such a distinguished scholar my friend. Thank you!"

"Just one more thing about McKinnley, he likes the element of surprise," Javier said.

I replied, "I remember that about him. He was always good a fighting from an ambush. I'll try to be ready for him."

Then almost as an afterthought, Javier said, "I heard that McKinnley's preferred way of taking someone down is cultivating a traitor within to betray his target. You might want to keep an eye on your staff."

I responded, "Although I hate the idea of doing that, I will take your warning under advisement, and I really appreciate your insight. Thank you!"

Javier stood to take his leave. We shook hands and said our goodbyes. As he left, he handed me an untraceable cell phone. "My number is programmed into this. Call me sometime. May God watch over you, my friend."

I hugged him and said, "You too, brother." He left me with a tear in his eye.

CHAPTER 36

I had a couple of really busy days, after which things slowed down a bit. I had wanted to go to the room behind the fireplace in order to check the cameras and set up a way to observe staff without spending all my time parked in front of those screens. A friend of mine who was a computer guru had come up with an algorithm that would key certain words that might indicate a conspiracy. Those words would key a message to my phone, and I could go check out that tape. It was a way of saving lots of time. So I went in and installed the program. If this worked like it was designed to do, it should give me a heads-up if something was brewing. It left me feeling a little dirty, but it seemed like the sensible solution at this point in time. If there was time to think it over and strategize, another idea may have presented itself, but this seemed like the best answer on short notice. I was surprised at how expensive it was, and my friend gave the friends and family price. Ouch!

While in the room, I was amazed at how neat and clean it was. There were no cobwebs or dust on anything. Even the fireplace, which was an exact carbon copy of the one in my office, was clean and polished. I wondered about that. Clearly somebody else knew about this place.

As I drove back to the office, another thought occurred to me. When I arrived, I went into Jennifer's office to talk with her. "Jennifer," I said, "there are some strange things going on and some dangerous people who are not happy with the work that Doc started and I have continued."

"I know," she replied in a subdued voice.

"There is something I want you to do for me," I said. "If there is ever a critically dangerous situation I will send you a message all in capital letters. If you ever receive an e-mail or text message from me in all capital letters, stop what you are doing and immediately leave the property. Do not wait. Do not respond to the message. Do not come into my office. Do you understand?"

"I do understand your order, but not your reasons," she replied.

I told her, "I'm going to tell you something that nobody on earth knows besides me, and now you. Doc did not die from a heart attack, he was poisoned. This was admitted to me by someone who has nothing to gain or lose by telling me. I had guessed it. He just admitted that I was correct. They may also try to kill me. I don't want you caught in their net. Do you understand that?"

"Yes!" she replied, "but I don't want to leave you hanging if something happens."

I replied to her, "Jennifer, the best thing that you can do is get off the property and call the authorities. Don't make the call until you are safe, but please make it. It could save my life. Okay?"

"Okay, I'll do it," she said.

She was visibly upset, so I asked her, "What is on your mind, Jennifer?"

"How did they poison Doc? He was very careful."

I replied, "Yes, he was careful, but they are very subtle."

"Well, do you know how they got to him?" she asked.

"I do know, but you might rather not know," I told her.

"What can that possibly mean?" she asked.

"Sometimes the truth is uglier than we can even imagine," I said.

"Okay, don't tell me, but I may ask at a later date," she said.

"If you really want to know, I will tell you. You would probably regret having asked, but I respect your integrity enough to be candid with you. All of this, though, is top secret. Nobody can know about it. Not even your husband. It would just endanger him, if he knew. Are you okay with that?" I said.

She looked at me slightly impishly. "I already have some things that I'm not permitted to share with anyone."

"Ah! So you're the one!" I said and walked out the door. I then knew that she knew the secret of the room behind the fireplace.

When I got back into my office, I scoured it, looking for a door that would lead into the room behind the office. It had to be there. I was sure that Jennifer did not go down to the boathouse and climb those stairs every time she needed to clean the office. The office looked like it was cleaned every week at the very least. I knew better than to ask her. It was clearly something Doc had told her was "top secret," and she was not going to divulge it even to me. I understood that. I would to the same thing. After more than an hour of going over the office inch by inch and pushing everything I could push and twisting every knob, I was no closer to finding the door. That was frustrating. Doc was a genius, and I was feeling very much like a dummy. I would go over it again with fresh eyes after a few days of giving it a rest.

On impulse, I decided to drive up to the airport near the lake where the plane was kept. An hour of two of soaring over the mountains seemed like a good idea. The drive up was uneventful. I found myself checking my rearview mirror. I hated feeling the need to do so, but it was almost natural for me. The training of years past began to kick in. I found myself checking my surroundings everywhere I went. Knowing who was behind the threat made me careful. McKinnley was no picnic under any circumstances. Caution was becoming the order of the day in my life. He probably didn't know about the plane. Doc's attorney did not even know about it.

Arriving at the airport, I enquired as to the correct hanger. The plane was a beautiful, two-engine Cessna. It looked like it couldn't wait to spring into the sky. After rolling the doors open, I rolled the plane out onto the concrete pad. I checked the maintenance records and noted that it had been checked just a few days before. The fuel tank was full. After the preflight check, I started the engines. They just purred. I was starting to feel excited. After being cleared by the tower, I took off. The plane was a dream to fly. It was fast and responsive. I loved flying it. As the hills and mountaintops rolled away below, my troubles just seemed to melt away as well. I flew south over Parkersburg and banked west into Southern Ohio and Northern Kentucky. Then I turned back north and headed back to my starting point. During the flight, I noted several other small airstrips within a short drive. Thinking that it might be prudent at some point to move the plane, I wanted to know where would be a good place to put it. Some other ideas started brewing in the back of my mind as well.

When I arrived back at the airstrip, it was time to eat. I stopped at the local diner and renewed my acquaintance with the people in there. I left word that I was in the market for a reliable, older pickup truck. Once during the drive back to Stone House, I found myself smiling for no apparent reason. It had been awhile since that had happened. I found both fishing and flying to be very therapeutic. Which reminded me, it had been awhile since I had been fishing. I needed to come back to the lake and take Doc's map out on the lake. I would do that soon or so I thought.

CHAPTER 37

Arriving back at Stone House, I checked my messages and, finding nothing pressing, I went into my suite to take a shower. I had lots to think about, so I grabbed a notepad and sat down in my recliner. I jotted down a list of what I knew for sure and then another of things that I strongly suspected based on what I knew. Then I made yet another list of things that could be but that I had no evidence whatsoever to support. Everything that I knew for sure made me believe that this was a very real plot. It was more like a plot inside a plot. The one was evident; the other probable, although not evident. What I knew was that somebody, some of whom I knew and others whom I did not know, were cloning the physical body of Jesus of Nazareth. At least they believed that they were. Some of the actors had good, although misguided, intentions. The master plot, not in clear evidence, was the very essence of evil.

Clones explained many of the nuances of the prophecies regarding the antichrist. For instance, the fact that the beast, although in the form of a man, is not called a man even though he is referred to as "he." It seems that the beast will be or appear to be a male human being. The fact that human beings born in the normal way become a living soul is clear. When a human being is cloned, however, an exact copy of the body is made, but whether or not the soul can be cloned is in question or even in doubt. Most orthodox theologians believe that a cloned human being would not be completely human, although there is no evidence one way or the other. The Bible does not discuss the issue, so there is no scriptural foundation for any of the available viewpoints. Another mystery explained by clones is the passage that says that the beast will suffer a head wound and all will presume him dead, but he will come back. It would be simple to replace one clone with another. It would, or at least could, be a seamless switch that would appear to be a miraculous resurrection from the dead. The public reaction would catapult the beast into a worldwide phenomenon. It would happen before the cameras of the world and would be broadcasted into homes all around the world. They would try to make Christians believe that it was the second coming of Christ physically. The beast, however, would not come as Jesus Christ, he would come in his own name as the new "messiah." I was pretty much convinced that the cloning part was right on.

I was not so sure as to how the mark of the beast would come about. One of the problems was that technology was changing so rapidly that today's newest would be obsolete in three months. I was quite sure that the general idea was right, but it would remain to be seen. Somewhere along the line, I fell asleep with my notepad on my lap. When I awakened, I was not alone in the room.

Something stirred and awakened me. When I opened my eyes, Sergeant McKinnley was sitting opposite me and grinning like a hyena.

"Sergeant!" I barked. "What are you doing here?"

He grinned at me and replied, "My job. I'm supposed to find out all you know, secure the journals that your predecessor left behind, and then shut you up in a most discrete and permanent way. I think I'm going to enjoy this, Major!"

The look in his eyes professed anything but joy. I was pretty sure that I was not going to enjoy it. "What time is it?" I asked.

"It's about zero six thirty," he replied. "What difference does it make, anyway?"

I said, "My secretary usually shows up at around seven thirty. Maybe I should call and give her the day off."

"Oh no, you don't," said McKinnley. "I really would love to meet her. She might have something interesting to say."

"She won't come into my office when she comes in unless I call her," I said. "I'll send her a message to come in and see me when she arrives."

"Good idea," he responded.

I quickly sent her this text: "JENNIFER, WHEN YOU ARRIVE THIS MORNING, COME DIRECTLY TO MY OFFICE. IMMEDIATELY!" McKinnley looked it over and gave it his okay. So I sent it. He said, "It's good that you did all caps. That makes it appear more emphatic."

"I'm glad you approve," I responded.

After a few minutes of sitting quietly, I offered to make coffee, to which McKinnley agreed. "Let's go to the kitchen," I said. "I could use some breakfast, how about you?"

"Yes, I'm hungry. What do you have to eat?" he asked.

"Almost any regular breakfast food you could want. Do you like pancakes? I make a mean corn meal pancake," I replied. "Are you alone or do you have people with you?"

He looked at me with a half grin and finally replied, "I have guys with me. They are guarding the doors so that we won't be disturbed."

I smiled at him and replied, "How thoughtful of them. Do you think they'll want some breakfast?"

"They are probably hungry too," he replied.

"Okay," I said, "I'll make an extra-large batch of pancakes and fry up about a dozen eggs. You might as well have them come in and eat breakfast with us. None of us are going anywhere for a while."

"How do you know that?" McKinnley asked.

"Oh, just an assumption on my part," I said. We walked to the kitchen, and I started the coffee pot and then mixed up a large batch of pancake batter.

When he called his men in, there were three of them and all armed. I figured McKinnley was armed although I could see no weapon on him. We were just finishing our breakfast when there was a knock at the door. McKinnley told me to answer it and just act like there was nothing going on. When I answered it, the police were there in force. There was what looked like a SWAT team backing the uniformed officer who knocked on the door. I immediately invited them in, and they asked if there was something wrong. I said, "There is definitely something wrong here, Officer. These men broke into my home and have been holding me prisoner since about six thirty this morning. They are not friends, nor did I invite them. There were sitting and watching me when I awakened today. I would like to have them charged and booked. The charges may be whatever you deem appropriate." I turned and glanced at McKinnley. He was standing there looking quite astounded. He was accustomed to being in charge, and suddenly he was not. It didn't set well with him. I noticed his men were glancing at each other with sardonic glances and half smiles. It appeared that they did not like him very well. "By the way, Officer," I continued, "this man is a war criminal and is wanted in Laos, Cambodia, and Kuwait for war crimes. I know for a fact that he is wanted in Kuwait for raping and killing a young boy during the First Gulf War. I'm sure there is paper on him somewhere. His name is McKinnley. The army will have records on him as well. He went AWOL to avoid prosecution for the charges in Kuwait. There may be a longer list of people who want him by now. He was under my command when the incident in Kuwait took place, so I have firsthand knowledge of that."

McKinnley's eyes were hating me about as hard as they could. I was not making friends, but I was disposing of enemies. They were going to have to find a new man to spearhead their anti-me campaign. I started chuckling. The officer looked at me with questioning eyes. "It's a matter that amuses me personally," I replied.

The police swept up the perpetrators and marched them out and to jail. They advised me that there would be a detective assigned and they would be in touch to secure a statement from me. I thanked them, and they left. I walked to Jennifer's office to find her sitting at her desk. I thanked her profusely for following the plan. It probably saved my life. At the very least, it saved me considerable misery. I also told her that she had been in some danger. They had wanted to question her, and that could be unpleasant.

CHAPTER 38

Sometime during the night, I awakened with this resolve. I was going to take a sabbatical to finish Doc's unfinished book. I had read the work that he had completed before passing and reviewed his notes and outlines for the subsequent chapters. He was a little over half done, but had detailed notes and outlines. All of the references were there, and he had all of the reference books in the library. Trust Doc to set it up so that it would be as easy as possible. I then dozed off for a couple more hours and got up in the wee hours of the morning.

After breakfast, I called an unscheduled meeting of the staff to let them know what I was planning. It was the only way I was going to be able to complete the book for Doc. Nobody seemed to object to the idea. Truthfully, the church hardly needed my guidance. I appointed the senior pastor to chair the board while I was gone. I also let the staff know that they were to respect his leadership as they would mine. They were pretty clear that power struggles would not be tolerated and troublemakers would not last long in the employ of Stone Church. A few heads dropped when I said that. I guess it was to be expected. They were also informed that

Jennifer would be sending me reports as frequently as necessary, but no less than weekly.

I started making personal preparations as well. There was no set date to get started, but I wanted everyone to know the plan in plenty of time. I was going to leave instructions with Jennifer that absolutely nobody but her was to enter my office or living quarters for any reason. The locks were changed, and she and I were the only ones with keys. I just did not trust people anymore and I hated being like that, but experience had taught me the wisdom of caution.

I also prepared a couple of go bags. One of them had Doc's journals, the bearer bonds, and the gold in it. The other had a few clothes and necessities packed. I was loading everything that I could on a laptop, which I kept with the go bags. I stashed them in my office. The journals and materials with them were stashed in the floor safe. My personal bag was in a cabinet so that it wasn't obvious. It was my plan to carefully plan the getaway, but part of that was being ready to go at a moment's notice…thus the go bags.

Over the next couple of weeks, I had several lengthy meetings with my senior staff and the senior pastor one on one. We had much to discuss. I did not tell him how to contact me. I told him that I would be in touch. I purchased several prepaid phones as I would leave my cell phone in my office when I left. It would be way too easy to track me by my cell phone.

Another thing that I did was spend time looking at small airports across the country. I wanted to be able to drop in and refuel without making much of a footprint. There would be a record, but untangling all of the details would take time. Once I was out of the USA, it would be next to impossible to track me. It took a bit of wrestling with myself to come to the realization that a strategic retreat was not running. Douglas MacArthur was a good reminder of that truth. My plans were to finish Doc's book, get it to the publisher, and then get back into the saddle. Maybe once the book was done, they would leave me alone.

When the attack came, it took me by surprise. The surprise was not that it came, but when and how it came. I walked into my office after lunch on a Friday afternoon to find Sergeant McKinnley sitting there. I looked at him in surprise and said, "I thought you were in jail!"

He chuckled. "What is the old saying? You can't keep a good man down?"

"Well," I replied, "although I agree with the sentiment, you don't qualify. It looks like your connections were more powerful than I anticipated."

He looked at me with pure hatred in his eyes. "I am out on bail, but the army is trying to decide what to do with me. The church is not going to hide me from them, so I still have those charges to face. They have had way too much negative publicity in the past few years to try to get me out of the country. Besides, hidden away, I'm no good to them."

I looked at him and asked, "What are you doing here?"

He replied in an ugly growl, "I came to finish what I started. I am going to beat you to death for reporting me to the army."

"You seem quite confident that you can do it," I replied evenly.

He laughed derisively. "You're an old man! I can take you in my sleep."

With that, he came at me and we went back and forth in the office. At first he was giving me all I could handle, and it appeared that he was getting the better of me. Then I changed tactics. I switched to some tricks that I had learned while in Israel sparring with the Mossad officers. I knocked him down two or three times. The last time, he got up very slowly. "I misjudged you," he said. "I'll be back. Don't try to run because I have armed guards of both of the doors." Then he walked out.

I looked around my office. It was a mess! My head was spinning as I stood in front of the fireplace with my back to it. I leaned back against the fireplace to rest a bit. As I did, something moved and it felt like the whole room was in motion. When I regained my bearings, I was still standing in front of the fireplace, but I was in the room behind the fireplace. Then it hit me. When Doc continually said and encouraged me to press the cross, he was not just talking about preaching, he was preparing me to use the escape route that he had set up. I quickly spun it around again and grabbed my two go bags. I then went back into the other room and sat down to watch the monitors. I called the police from the phone in there and then called Jennifer. She answered and told me that when she came back from lunch, she saw men loitering around the building and did not even go in. She just left. It told her that she did exactly the right thing. I asked her if she knew about the fireplace. She said that Doc had showed it to her. She had been keeping it clean all this time. I told her she was a number 1 secret keeper, and she laughed. I also told her that the police were on the way to pick up those who had attacked.

While I was talking to Jennifer, Sergeant McKinnley came back into my office. He stopped in his tracks and stared around the office. He then called his guards from the hallway and my bedroom. He let them have it, but they both told him that I had not come out through there. Then he thought that I must have a hiding place in the office. He opened every door and tried every knob and lever looking for a secret panel or something. By the time he had covered the entire office, he was furious and it was about to get worse. My monitors showed the police had arrived in force and were coming in through the office and the residence, as I had instructed them to do. They burst into my office from both doors at the same time. Their weapons were pointed at the sergeant. They took three firearms off him. He really had come back to finish me. He wouldn't be making bail this time, I thought.

I went down the stairs to the boathouse and loaded my stuff in the launch. I opened the door to the boathouse and headed slowly down the channel to the river. At the marina, I left the boat in their care and picked up a car that I had stashed close by. I had made several plans of escape, and one of them had been by boat. I had no idea that Doc was going to make that so easy for me. I drove up to the airport where Doc had left the plane. When I left the house, I had left my old cell phone behind. I called the airport on one of my new prepaid phones and ordered the plane prepped. When I arrived there, I pulled my car into the hanger. They already had the plane out and ready to go. I filed a flight plan to Birmingham, Alabama, did my preflight, and took off. Once I was out of the tower control, I veered off and headed west. My first stop was at a small airfield is southern Missouri. I had served in spec ops with the owner, so I could count on his discretion. He also knew McKinnley. I was pretty sure that he had not sympathy for him. I landed finally at a small, private airport near Conroe, Texas. I was going home to Texas for a while. I would not live in my home as it was rented. I had lots of contacts in Texas and was pretty sure that I would be able to finish Doc's book in the next few months. Maybe by then the heat would be off and I could go back to Stone Church.